Architecture Profile 4
SHAY CLEARY ARCHITECTS

Published as part of Gandon Editions'
PROFILES series on Irish architects
(details p131).

ISBN 0946846 898

Editor   John O'Regan

Asst Editor   Nicola Dearey
Design   John O'Regan
                (© Gandon Editions, 2002)
Production   Nicola Dearey, Sheila Holland
                @ Gandon Editions
                Gunther Berkus
Printing   Nicholson & Bass, Belfast

Distributed by Gandon and its overseas agents

GANDON EDITIONS
Oysterhaven, Kinsale, Co Cork, Ireland

tel   +353 (0)21-4770830
fax   +353 (0)21-4770755
e-mail   gandon@eircom.net
web-site   www.gandon-editions.com

Publication grant-aided by
The Arts Council / An Chomhairle Ealaíon
and assisted by
The Royal Institute of the Architects of Ireland

Dedication   for Lulu, Ben, Oliver
                and Annabel

Photography   John Searle

                additional photography by
                Bill Hastings – 26bl, 27-28,
                30t, 30bl, 33, 35, 70, 116b,
                117
                Shay Cleary Architects – 16t,
                38-41, 128

Models   Tom Larkin

                additional models by
                Stephen Musiol (Blackrock
                Education Centre, Deputy
                Master's House, Glandore Road)

cover   Cork County Hall (1999-)
frontispiece   Arthouse, Temple Bar, Dublin
                (1992-95)

Profile

Shay Cleary Architects

GANDON EDITIONS

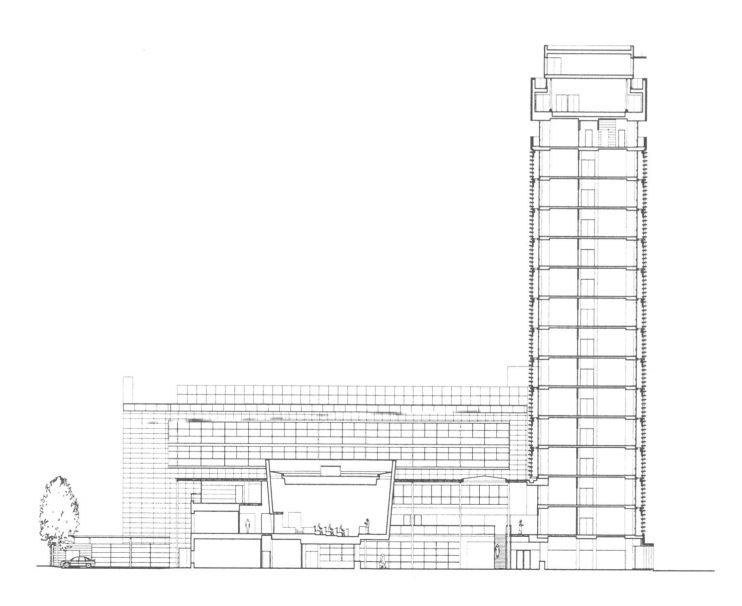

Contents

Redevelopment and Extension of Cork County Hall (1999-)

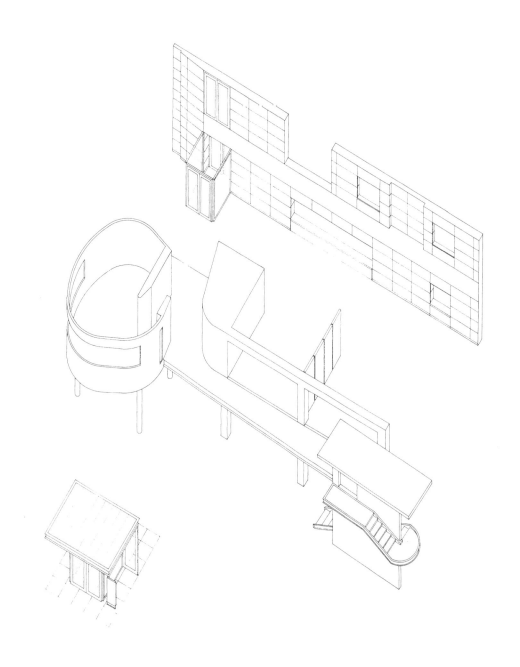

Order + Incident

An Irish Constructivism

RAYMUND RYAN

In ancient Ireland and in Irish vernacular architecture, buildings were typically massive. Robust, often squat, in general opaque. With the Enlightenment, and with the arrival of architecture as a profession, delicate and taut façades began to appear in the Irish Georgian streetscape. The number of windows in these façades was determined by legal and practical as well as formal concerns. Daylight was of course required for sensible interior illumination, but 18th-century designers were also conscious of these new urban walls as an aesthetic construct. Although architecture is often considered as a matter of isolated objects, the architecture of Dublin was characterised by this refinement of communal surface.

Shay Cleary is unmistakably a Modernist, an architect in that progressive, sometimes stark lineage integrally associated with 20th-century culture but instigated very much earlier. With his exploration of volume and structure and colour, Cleary has been inspired by the urbane and painterly work of Le Corbusier (1887-1965). Indebted to the Swiss-French master, the Irish architect's work has nevertheless developed its own local resonance. Its methodology of form, structure and skin has some Classical essence akin – albeit in the materials of today – to the thin architecture and luminous interiors of the Enlightenment. Georgian Dublin did not develop

Meeting & Conference Facilities,
Dept of Agriculture, Dublin (1993-94)

7

organically: Irish neo-Classicism was itself an adaptation of European modes and theories of design.

Until recently, this historic fabric suffered from extraordinary neglect and dereliction. With suburbia expanding outwards in unplanned spasms, medieval, Georgian and Victorian Dublin has been the site of much insensitive building and of traffic engineering imposed in the name of progress. A typical response is to resort to imagery, to create a sort of Potemkin Village of illiterate reproduction. Cleary's Dublin work results instead from a vivid Modernism, an approach to design which may paradoxically be closer in spirit to Dublin's historic cityscape than today's generic kitsch. Cleary introduces new veils and membranes in between the old, skins of a lightness and sensuousity unimaginable to Georgian builders dependent upon load-bearing masonry.

Cleary shares the 'conviction' noticed by Alan Colquhoun – in the work of the New York Five – 'that the "new tradition" of avant-garde art constituted a historical development from which it was impossible to turn back'.[1] He is enamoured with Modernism but tackles many of the shortcomings of 1960s international corporatist design. He is both inquisitive about his architecture's own stylistic roots and alert to complex issues of urbanism and meaning, issues mostly ignored during the period of his own professional training. In Ireland today, Cleary develops the cosmopolitan language of radically inventive modernist architects to address evolving realities of construction, urban development and institutional representation.

RETURN TO THE CITY I

Why might an Irish architect of Cleary's generation be drawn to what Americans call the International Style? After all, in his manifesto *The City of To-Morrow*, Le Corbusier had declared that 'surgery must be applied at the city's centre …wide avenues must be driven through …the existing centres must come down'.[2]

The Irish Free State never really embraced Modernity. In such

important commissions as Dublin's Busáras, Michael Scott (1905-1989) managed however to introduce new themes of construction, programmation and expression from the continent. In later decades, Scott's partners Ronald Tallon and Robin Walker (1924-1991) achieved impressive singular buildings (RTÉ studios, Donnybrook; Bank of Ireland Headquarters, Dublin) intimately inspired by the North American work of Mies van der Rohe (1886-1969). The critical difference between these earlier generations and architects such as Cleary is the latter's attitude towards history and context.

Shay Cleary graduated from University College Dublin in 1974, then left for Paris, Walter Benjamin's 'capital of the nineteenth century', the crucible of early Modern experimentation and achievement. In Paris he worked in the offices of Marcel Breuer (1902-1981) and Candilis Josic Woods (the former a Hungarian-born star Bauhaus pupil who created a robust organic style; the latter a collaborative attempting to tune methods of mass production to the construction of humane, democratic environments). But High Modernism – the Modernism of La Défense, the Modernism made fun of in films by Jacques Tati – came under scrutiny by younger architects in the early 1970s. In London, in Paris, in Milan, they began to re-evaluate the nature and significance of existing cities.

As has been documented in Frank McDonald's *The Destruction of Dublin*, and as Dubliners over thirty may still recollect, the city to which Cleary returned in the late 1970s was in seemingly terminal decay. The Dublin McDonald describes has 'an almost dead city centre' where 'dereliction is positively encouraged while responsible conservation is penalised'.[3] In 1980, as part of the Independent Artists' exhibition, a dozen or so architects presented proposals for contemporary façades on generic Georgian plots. Between neo-vernacular and more overtly Postmodernist tendencies, Cleary envisaged a geometric mask with both studio-type vitrines and double-height cut-outs revealing a recessed inner layer, an accumulative, abstract language for communal habitation reminiscent of Le Corbusier's Esprit Nouveau apartments of 1925.

In a culture either careless about its fabric or afflicted with

doubt as to how to build in an appropriate way, Cleary's design maintained the prospect of a civil contemporary architecture. In the late 1970s, Cleary worked with Yvonne Farrell, Frank Hall, Shelley McNamara and Tony Murphy in the practice which they founded, known as Grafton Architects. A few years later, in partnership with Hall, he realised three subtle mews houses in a lane off Upper Leeson Street. In fact the three adjacent court-yard houses, with their high outer gables and a communal colonnade *in antis*, essentially define that lane. In these urban pieces, Cleary linked an analysis of typology with abstract visual composition, a respect for context maintained in such later works as the Scoop House in Rathmines.

A decade after the Independent Artists' exhibition – in 1991, Dublin's year as European City of Culture – many of the same architects again joined forces to propose a row of high-density, mixed-use dwellings in Dublin's inner city.[4] That somewhat eclectic scheme for South Earl Street in the Liberties was never realised. However Cleary, his former partners Farrell and McNamara, and several of their fellow instructors from UCD School of Architecture pushed their collaborative potential fur-ther. Later that same year, Group 91 – a collective of eight prac-tices including Shay Cleary Architects – was awarded first prize for its Temple Bar Framework Plan.[5] Having inserted smaller architectural projects as constituent fragments into the urban grain, Cleary was now in a position to confidently help reconfig-ure the capital city.

RETURN TO THE CITY II

The Temple Bar Framework Plan was in certain ways conserva-tive. Rather than demolition, or erecting brutally tall structures above much lower neighbours, Group 91's urbanistic ambition was to weave new fragments or swatches of building through the warehouses, backyards and disused religious institutions of Temple Bar. The plan also entailed giving priority to the pedes-trian experience within the city district. In deliberate defiance of the transport interchange proposed by Skidmore Owings & Merrill in the 1980s, and the ensuing problems of both physical bulk and motorised traffic, Group 91 envisaged three new

Scoop House, Rathmines, Dublin (1999-2000)　　　　　Making a Modern Street (1991)

squares and one short new street divined out of existing conditions – public urban spaces from which the automobile would be banned.

Today, Curved Street connects Temple Bar Square and the arched tunnel leading into Meeting House Square and onwards to East Essex Street. Unlike the glory days of the 18th century, it is most unusual for contemporary architects to have the chance to design an entire street. For Modernists, with their cult of open space, the very idea of an enclosed street was anathema. Here in Dublin in the 1990s, Curved Street was formed by two distinct buildings – the Temple Bar Music Centre by McCullough Mulvin and Arthouse by Shay Cleary. That's also unusual, that a single building might define one entire side of a thoroughfare. With an international and vanguard language, Cleary's building also adjusts itself to accommodate its neighbours.

Arthouse occupies the south side of the street. Its great concave façade of smooth white plaster is a screen perforated with many different forms of opening. At street level, passers-by are met with a barrage of video and audio equipment as if the architect has fused his abstract, geometric inclinations with more social, democratic intent ('high' architecture accommodating the ad hoc liveliness of media equipment stores, DVD rental outlets and possibly even the nightclub). In the elevation above, sliding double-height doors allow views into a cubic eyrie, a high void in the urban mass laced through with open steel stairs, the bones of exposed structure, and the glazed shaft of a freestanding elevator. With its installation of kinetic service elements, this protected space shares an informality with the courtyard envisaged for South Earl Street.

Discovered inside the veiled cage of circulation systems and more self-contained conference and technical rooms is an entire house, a comparatively minor 19th-century dwelling facing onto Eustace Street, now punctured to serve as a secondary exhibition space at ground floor, with administration above. It is a rather gallant accommodation, by Cleary, of the old within the new. 'The curving street is essentially picturesque,' Le Corbusier had written in *The City of To-Morrow*, 'a pleasure which quickly becomes boring if too frequently gratified'.

Arthouse on Curved Street, Temple Bar, Dublin (1992-95)

Project Arts Centre, Temple Bar, Dublin (1996-2000)

Remembering the Modernist's 1920s injunction that 'Surgery must be applied at the city's centre, Physic must be used elsewhere', one wonders whether today the inverse is not true.

It is perhaps inherent to the fledgling nature of communication technologies and associated art practices that the Arthouse programme is constantly evolving. Beneath a glazed roof, the light-filled upper space is home to a rather informal cyber café. Looking back over Curved Street, beneath the flange of a cantilevered hoist, one sees through another glazed gap in the convex Music Centre opposite to a raised linear courtyard at the heart of the Printworks project (Derek Tynan Architects). These connections – through both accumulative mass and subtractive voids – are intrinsic to Group 91's holistic vision of the city. The complexity achieved by Cleary recalls Kepes' remark that 'transparency means a simultaneous perception of different spatial locations'.[6]

On from Curved Street, funnelled through the eclectic Meeting House Square, the pedestrian comes to East Essex Street and the cubistic façade of the new Project Arts Centre. It is faced in vivid blue render and matt metal panels. On this same site since the 1970s, the Project was determined to retain, with the benefit of increased funding and a distinguished architect, its location in Temple Bar and a pragmatic multi-functionalism. Thus Cleary designed metal garage doors giving directly onto the street, a 'shop window' vitrine exposing the lower foyer, and two performance spaces intentionally considered as black boxes (offering directors, designers, sound and light engineers ultimate flexibility). There's a long foyer/bar serving the principal performance space on the *piano nobile*, with staff offices and a generous terrace above offering syncopated views across the adjacent rooftops. This tiered, practical architecture is stacked up towards the north, as if a segment of an ocean-going liner had somehow docked in the narrow Dublin street.

JUXTAPOSING OLD AND NEW

In the 1970s, New York witnessed an ambitious reworking of Le Corbusier's early machine aesthetic. Le Corbusier's output divides into two principal sections: the International Style (with its predilection for ideal geometry and transatlantic liners) and a more emotional post-War phase (labelled Brutalism due to its fondness for raw concrete – *concret brut*). It was to the earlier period that certain young Americans looked, to the Le Corbusier who proclaimed 'geometry is the means, created by ourselves, whereby we perceive the external world and express the world within us', to Le Corbusier whose dazzling collages grafted columns, segments of wall, and curvaceous room modules into 1920s Paris. Gathered together as *Five Architects* in 1972, the group drew on the abstract linguistic character of Le Corbusier's compositions. In his introduction to their influential catalogue, Arthur Drexler wrote of 'a teachable vocabulary of forms' and 'an architecture of rational poetry'.[7] The group – Peter Eisenman, Michael Graves, Charles Gwathmey, John Hejduk and Richard Meier – went on to achieve critical influence and success, particularly in the construction of art museums. In the late 1970s Alan Colquhoun described a design by Graves as 'a balanced asymmetrical whole', words appropriate to Cleary's complex but less pedantic or arcane work in subsequent decades.

The interplay between the orthogonal and the free-form (in Meier's case, typically a grand piano shape) develops through Cleary's career to become one of contrast between free-standing building blocks. At the Blackrock Education Centre, an oval pavilion sets up a gentle tension by being slightly off-axis with regard to the attendant built mass. At Blackrock, on a nondescript suburban site, Cleary also evokes the pure internalised cloister of ancient religious and educational settlements. In competition proposals for Dun Laoghaire Rathdown County Hall and the Science of Materials Building at Trinity College Dublin, he establishes arrays of slim office accommodation against which non-orthogonal elements are arranged as plastic accents.

The National Centre for Irish Language Education about to start on site at Ballyvourney, west Cork, develops these themes of order and incident. Its linear system gathers smaller spaces containing washrooms and stairs along an extended northern wall, whilst articulating communal areas as a pavilion towards the south. From this wall, the library and boardroom splay out as a volumetric incident. To the south, the principal seminar room expands upwards into a closed cubic form above an open, glazed foyer. Less Corbusian than Cleary's earlier work, Ballyvourney also represents an evolving interest in the possibilities of new materials. It is to be clad in laminated timber panels, increasing the sleek planarity of vertical exterior surfaces.

Extensions to the Wall House, the official residence of the president of Dublin City University, are also reminiscent of certain moves by both the New York Five and, much earlier, Ludwig Mies van der Rohe. The common theme is the exploration of walls, the extension of vertical surfaces – in this case, yellow brick – out across a lawn, subdividing the site into sensitively screened zones. Mies's unbuilt Brick Villa project first presented this dynamic strategy in 1923. (It was in turn influenced by the Dutch neo-Plasticist / de Stijl movement, including works by the painters van Doesburg and Mondrian.) Cleary's inclusion in the formal dining room of a white silk curtain parallel to a wall of red plaster seems to be a deliberate homage to Mies's luxurious pavilion for the Weimar Republic at Barcelona in 1929.

The hybridity of the Wall House is closer however to the knowing exercises of the New York Five: it is contingent on the integration of existing fragments. Cleary's walls and roofs extend outward from a homely Victorian lodge so that the old becomes a fulcrum for the new. Although a smaller guest pavilion in the south lawn has yet to be constructed, the older ashlar villa with its pitched roofs and rustic porch acts as the central pivot of this small arcadian universe.

Unlike those of Mies, but like the street façade or mask of Cleary's earlier Box House in Sandymount, these new walls have some figuration. One punched opening recalls the famous patio 'window' built by Le Corbusier for his mother to overlook Lake Geneva. The entire site is to be bordered in a dense hedge – linear *poché* – to create an external green room. The floor-to-ceiling glass membranes, the most obvious recollection of Mies, will thus benefit from interaction between bands of vegetation, clear glass and opaque walls.

Affinities with New York Five geometric strategies are further manifested at the Deputy Masters' House, Kilmainham. Cleary has renovated that four-square, 18th-century mass as an exhibition and curatorial facility. The attic has been stripped down to skin and structure, and lightbox monitors introduced to help bridge the valley between parallel pitched roofs, so that the stairwell now extends upwards to a view of historic timber trusses crisscrossing in a zone lined with Cleary's clean white walls. This spirit of engagement with and revelation of an existing structural and spatial context shares a pleasure in assemblage with Graves's Gunwyn Investment Office (Princeton, 1972) and with John Hejduk's magisterial refurbishment of Cooper Union in Manhattan in the mid-1970s.

The curvilinear mezzanine inserted by Cleary in 1993 into the double-height hall of Agriculture House presents this post-Corbusian language to Irish civil servants, farmer representatives and passers-by on Dublin's Kildare Street. It's a play on geometry, floating a studied biomorphic shape and open, bull-nose stairs away from the orthogonal grid of that rather dreary 1970s office building. And it's a subtly volumetric device, swelling forward into a previously little-noticed space, bright yellow, unlike any other visible surface, engaging the void in a dialectical way so that now one depends on the other for its architectural resonance or meaning. According to Cleary, the mezzanine is shaped to facilitate views of a Patrick Scott tapestry on the foyer's end wall.

To many Dubliners, infuriated or simply made to feel helpless by the annihilation of urban fabric as described by McDonald, it may appear paradoxical that old buildings might be saved, rejuvenated and made useful again by that same International Modernism held accountable for so many negative decisions between World War II and the economic recession of the early 1980s. By the second decade of Cleary's career, the priority given to clarity and light (a priority dear to the Georgians but sidelined by subsequent generations) re-emerged in an unprecedented admiration for old industrial structures. Warehouses were colonised by artists and then by young urban fashionables as lofts (from *luft*, or air).

In 1989, Cleary's work at the Point Depot, a former railroad

Irish Museum of Modern Art, Royal Hospital Kilmainham, Dublin (1990-91)

New Galleries, Irish Museum of Modern Art, Dublin (1995-99)

loading facility in Dublin's docklands, brought him the Downes Medal from the Architectural Association of Ireland. Distilling architecture to envelope and structure, Cleary inserted a metal mezzanine down the length of the double-height hall, allowing for unexpected views – ludic knowledge – both out to the Liffey and in among the building elements themselves. This elegant and, at the time, somewhat startling renovation serviced a bar and restaurant. The loft or warehouse had emerged as a new interior model. Cleary's feeling for light and space subsequently found its richest expression in associated projects for gallery and exhibition spaces.

BUILDING FOR ART

The Royal Hospital Kilmainham might be described as a proto-Modernist artifact, a manifestation in stone of the three classical categories of knowledge: memory, imagination and reason. It is a pure form of sorts, a square courtyard with enclosing walls of stone, set amid acres of lush parkland on the fringes of Dublin's inner city. Used as a storage depot after Irish independence in 1921, the hospital was restored with fanfare in the early 1980s. A decade later, the 300-year-old building was chosen to house a newly invented institution, the Irish Museum of Modern Art. As IMMA's first director Declan McGonagle stated at the gala opening one sunny afternoon in 1991, the institution's aspiration is to question all four words of its title.

The museum inhabits three of the four sides of the flat courtyard – the first room of the museum in Cleary's mind. The primary visible intervention is in one central hallway (the other two lead directly to the surrounding parkland) where the architect orientates the visitor about a pristine grand stairs made of stainless steel and hovering glass threads. Upstairs, exhibition spaces extend down broad, airy corridors or lodge in bedrooms formerly shared by military retirees but now connected one to the next by paired doorways. Technical apparatuses are discreetly dispersed throughout the resuscitated fabric of the hospital.

Cleary's later renovation of the adjacent Deputy Master's House is an accomplished supplementary project. This building reappears, Lazarus-like, from its slumber towards the edge of the immediate hospital precinct. Externally, the grafting of a ramp and stone walls make an entrance and sunny terrace on the roof of the new basement gallery (which extends below, beyond the curtilage of the historic structure). But these are more than stylish accoutrements offering, as it happens, an enticing view over the restored gardens towards the Liffey. These fragments of construction mark the north-east corner of the museum's built terrain. They are axial coordinates, suggesting a contemporary redefinition of a formally structured site.

Having first met with some foreign competition success at Durham's Oriental Museum in 1984, Cleary was again runner-up thirteen years later in a competition for Walsall Art Gallery in the English Midlands. For this location at a canal terminus in a rather shabby, post-industrial town, Cleary proposed a three-sided figure of orthogonal blocks and one almost miniature tower. The three wings enclose a courtyard visible through glazed openings from the adjacent shopping streets. In turn, it looks back down and frames the canal. For Walsall, Cleary furthermore proposed the superimposition of static and kinetic images integrated into the architecture as another set of orthogonal elements. But the main room of the gallery is the exterior space 'discovered' in the contemporary urban maze.

RETURN TO THE CITY III

In the 1980s, Cleary's aspiration to consider the city as a Work of Art (a concept dear to Aldo Rossi and much earlier urbanists such as Camillo Sitte) may have seemed farfetched and unlikely to succeed. In Dublin in 2002, it seems almost accepted as a fact of life.

Next to the Mansion House with its recessed forecourt on Dawson Street, the most prototypical of Cleary's recent projects is currently nearing completion. This is an office building – that most mundane of programmes and the cause of much urban destruction in the 1960s and 1970s. If his intervention at Agriculture House used supermodernist forms to liberate certain latent spatial qualities, the building on Dawson Street wraps

space with carefully composed orthogonal skins. It abstracts the fenestration of previous centuries into a new pattern of 'punched' openings, then breaks the building mass in two so that that towards the Mansion House decreases in height.

Connecting to the flat bay windows or oriels along Dawson Street, the building's forward portion is clad in red sandstone with subtly proportioned fenestration. As the massing defers to the ceremonial presence of the Mansion House, the walls change to paler limestone, the openings become vertical. Across from the mayor's dining room, Cleary introduces a projecting quadripartite serrated window to direct views from inside the office space out towards the public street. Like that of Alvar Aalto (1898-1976) in several understated but elegant buildings in central Helsinki, this is a Modernism unusually sensitive to location. Unlike disconnected office buildings of the recent past, Cleary's is contiguous with and subsidiary to the urban realm.

If Cleary's work in Dawson Street extends the urban wall as a stereometric curtain, his public housing at Queen Street – at a different place in the socio-economic spectrum – reinserts the urban villa to line a formal public space. It also integrates the debased Modernism of four existing housing slabs into an urban block simultaneously defined and perforated. The new construction consists of three and four-storey 'houses' containing apartments, with individual external stairways and terraces. Painted terracotta along their Queen Street façades, these units collectively instigate a bold rhythm of solid and void through which the older slab buildings are glimpsed and the interior terrain accessed.

The Queen Street reorganisation promotes a domestically scaled, spatial architecture distinct from the privatised behemoths of Celtic Tiger 'developments'. Cleary's chain of villas allows light and air – as well as views – in and around each residential unit. This strategy of additive types, reminiscent of Le Corbusier's worker housing at Pessac near Bordeaux, is complemented in the refurbishment of the older apartments on the site. There the horizontal circulation system of access decks is being replaced by external group stairs. Whereas low walls will configure the open ground plane into more comprehensible or identifiable zones, Cleary also proposes to clip trellises onto the south-facing elevations to provide shade and a generally less naked appearance.

This reintroduction of Modernism into the fabric of Dublin is clearly symbolised in Cleary's unpremiated proposal to find a successor object to the demolished Nelson's Pillar, that giant pivotal column or *axis mundi* once ascending to a panoramic deck above the roofs of Joyce's Hibernian metropolis. He envisaged a translucent vitreous shaft, square in plan, rising from below pavement level up towards a clear glass cube floating in the skies above the General Post Office. Cleary had previously proposed an embedded glass cube (today's futurist equivalent of the domes or hemispheres of the Enlightenment?) for the National Gallery extension onto Clare Street.

Some trace of Cleary's Constructivist project (the competition judges rejected any wish for a contemporary viewing terrace) reappears in the tower being reconstructed on Dublin's Grand Canal Quay. Reducing each floor (very small in plan) to essential office-space requirements, the architect is adding a supplementary thin tower – a vertical frame – housing elevators and stairs, with a skeletal cube as a penthouse finale. There is some poignancy, perhaps, that this addition in a newly affluent Irish setting occurs close to the former site of the Retort Building, a taut, anonymous artifact with passing resemblance to constructions of the Russian avant-garde.

With his competition-winning design for Cork County Hall, scheduled to begin construction in late 2002, Shay Cleary's reintegration of Modernism into Irish architecture comes full circle. In Cork he deals with an unprepossessing inheritance from the 1960s – the tallest but certainly not the finest building in Ireland. A new skin of glass louvres will sheath the tower slab, dematerialising its bulk as a vitreous volume while also offering climatic protection. At ground level the complex is integrated with the public world by the addition of a generous open hall containing a singular ovoid council chamber. In this important undertaking for the architect and the county, there are also the beginnings of an ecological sophistication.

In his introduction to *Five Architects*, Arthur Drexler wrote of a post-Corbusian 'architecture of rational poetry'. Irish architecture of the 18th century shared some of those characteristics. Today however, in our increasingly complex, hybrid and heterogeneous times, architecture must adapt and integrate. The architecture of Shay Cleary moves along these vectors of idealism and empirical response. Radically informed by the aspirations and materials of the 20th century, it recalls Laszlo Moholy-Nagy's comment about Joyce 'building up a completeness by an ingenious transparency of relationships'. In Cleary's work, relationships serve a new communal understanding of environment.

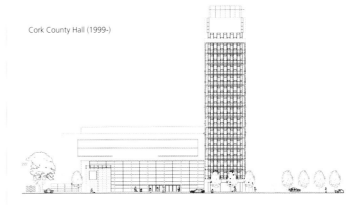

Cork County Hall (1999-)

Raymund Ryan teaches at the School of Architecture, UCD. He is co-author of *Building Tate Modern* (Tate Publishing, London, 2000), and author of *Cool Construction* (Thames & Hudson, London, 2001).

ENDNOTES

1 Alan Colquhoun, 'From Bricolage to Myth, or how to put Humpty-Dumpty together again', *Oppositions* (New York, 1979)
2 Le Corbusier, *The City of To-Morrow* (Architectural Press, London 1947; originally published as *Urbanisme*, 1924)
3 Frank McDonald, *The Destruction of Dublin* (Gill & Macmillan, Dublin, 1985)
4 *Making a Modern Street: An Urban Proposal for Dublin* (Gandon Editions, 1991)
5 See *Temple Bar: The Power of an Idea* (Temple Bar Properties, Dublin, 1996)
6 Colin Rowe & Robert Slutzky, 'Transparency: Literal and Phenomenal', *Perspecta*, no. 8 (New Haven, 1963)
7 *Five Architects* (New York, 1975)

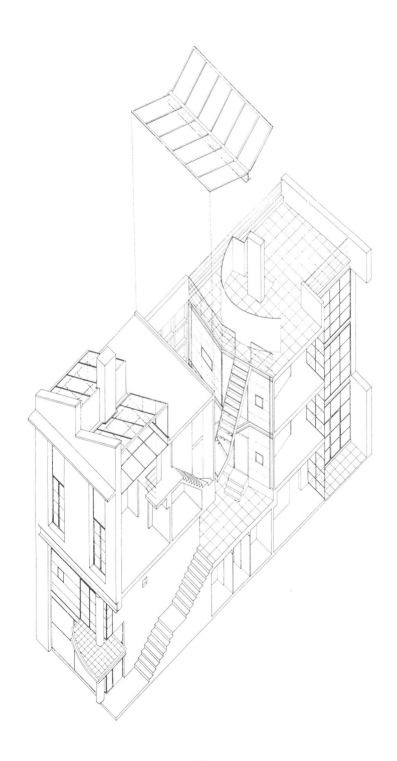

Making a
New Reality

INTERVIEW BY SIMON WALKER

Simon Walker – Shay, you've been in practice for over twenty years. Let's talk about your beginnings as an architect. Were you always interested in architecture?

Shay Cleary – No, I decided on the spur of the moment. I was going to be an engineer but I didn't get the right results in my Leaving – I didn't get honours in maths. My father, in his innocence, said to me, 'Well, why don't you do architecture instead? It's the same thing isn't it?' I went to UCD and did fairly well in first and second year, although at the time it didn't mean that much to me. Then in third year I was taught by the 'Flying Circus' of Ed Jones, Mike Gold, Chris Cross and Fenella Dixon. Their message was essentially that architecture was an incredibly exciting world to do with ideas and making space, and they made it extremely engaging. I got fired up by it then, and I thought yes, it would be amazing to be an architect. We had reviews of work which were fantastically provocative because they are extremely articulate people. That really got me going.

You went to work with Marcel Breuer in Paris.

Making a Modern Street, Dublin (1991)

In college, a certain group of us were friends – Yvonne [Farrell], Shelley [McNamara] and Tony [Murphy] – and that friendship was associated with work as well. Tony and I, along with Eugene Dunne, decided to go to Paris, primarily because of Le Corbusier's work. Corb had died, but we went there on a pilgrimage of sorts. A tutor in third year, Paul Moore, gave us an introduction to Mario Jossa, who ran Marcel Breuer's office in Paris. We went to see him and he gave us a job that afternoon. It was very exciting as young architects to be in a famous architect's office. I worked there for about six months.

They must have been able to read your enthusiasm for Corb's work.

I think so, yes. It also created a certain amount of friction. We wanted to be given a free hand, which in most design offices is a very unreal sort of aspiration, and we had great rows, but always in a very positive way. Mario Jossa was a very benign boss who humoured us. We had also been interested in the Berlin Free University, which was a very controversial project that Candilis, Josic & Woods had done, so after six months Tony and I went to work with Candilis. Shadrac Woods was dead at that stage. What we met was a kind of production factory full of Japanese people.

That kind of practice must have been a big change from the domestic scene.

Well, the irony was that we were given very large projects to look at. I mean, we were asked to develop plans for a range of schools in Saudi Arabia, and off we went and produced mini-Berlin Free Universities – a type of grid plan with linear circulation, big spaces down the middle, and small spaces at the sides. And Candilis hated it all. He had obviously fallen out of love with that way of doing things at some stage, and suddenly he had two Irish guys in the corner producing work that he wasn't into anymore. He was into clusters; we were into linear developments. Woods had said somewhere that 'a point is static, a line is a measure of freedom', but Candilis had gone back to making clusters, and we were saying no, no, you must make these movement patterns. All of which was all very interesting until he fired us.

Swan Place, off Upper Leeson Street, Dublin
(Cleary & Hall, 1983)

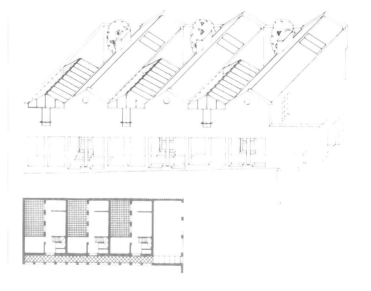

Did this non-site-specific work enable you to develop a kind of international language when you came back to Ireland?

Well, I suppose we used it to a certain degree. I mean, we had been working on large projects, so when we came back to Ireland we were trying to make it relevant to our own place, while at the same time looking over our shoulder at international developments, and believing that that was a good way to be.

Did you feel an imperative to look for a new language in response to conditions here?

When we founded Grafton Architects in 1978, yes, we felt there was a necessity to do that, because the options here were quite limited. We weren't interested in the Mies thing, although as one gets older one finds a powerful kind of understanding in that work. We were interested in a more volumetric and spatially elaborate architecture. We started our own practice because we didn't want to work for anyone else, and we were also inspired by the Flying Circus. They had shown that a group of young architects could work successfully together, and that was very useful for a number of years.

There is a tendency in so-called High Modernism to inflate the importance of language, to often use empiricism seemingly without the benefit of reason.

The complexity can be there, but I believe a certain kind of stillness is important. I'm always trying to make things that aren't 'fashionable'. Even though somebody may believe that it fits into a kind of category, my aim is to make work that doesn't date. I think a project needs to deal with the problem at hand, but also say something at a general level. You're making a statement, but not in loud way.

Is that also your approach to urbanism?

I think it is. A significant project for me was Swan Place. It was the first building that I built. I was in practice with Frank Hall at the time. What interested me was that there seemed to be little value placed on secondary streets and lanes – road engineers saying that you had to have a certain set-back because these streets might be widened at some stage, resulting in the general destruction of the street wall. In Swan Place, necessities of the site meant that the houses were placed right on the street, and I spent six months trying to make a plan that was ingenious at getting round the constrictions of the site, and at the same time remake the street edge. The idea that there might be both a general and a specific aim remains a goal for me.

You have talked about the façade as a mediator in relation to Arthouse and to the Project. The Arthouse façade delineates the street and also reveals the elements within, while the Project façade models the outdoor space. It's a different kind of theatre.

The primary architectural move in Arthouse was to make the concave plane which was then inhabited with various uses, like another layer behind it. It has a basic symmetry, but the elements within it are in a much more open play. It was interesting because it didn't matter what you did once you had made that primary move.

The Project Arts Centre is indicative of the urban condition in an interesting way. Because of the highly restricted nature of the site, all of the service and back-of-house uses coexist with the front-of-house, so you have the main entrance and the scene-dock entrance together on the front. It describes a very contemporary urban condition, which is that you've got limited space to work with. We couldn't go down because of the Poddle River, we couldn't go up because of planning restrictions, so everything gravitates to the front, and that becomes the palette of events which you have to deal with.

Arthouse is more to do with the void in the urban block. You are generally comfortable with insertion projects.

I think if you have a context you get your clues from that. It helps you to make those steps. It's much more difficult to do a building out in a field.

The insertion works go back as far as the Point Depot. You had a powerful existing shell, and your response to that was to make a very simple, formal device as counterpoint.

Yes, the contrast between the rough limestone walls and the precise steel interventions made for an interesting atmosphere.

The Point is so indisputable and symmetrical. Was there a nervousness at that time, in the mid-eighties, about stepping into that kind of formalist territory?

Well, the Point was difficult because there was a decision made – which I thought was crazy – that the main entrance should be away from the riverside. The planners felt that with people spilling out the front it would be too dangerous. So we inserted two bars joined by a bridge, and then joined together again when you got above the double-height space, with the restaurant on the top. So it was an odd kind of abstract project in one way. I was primarily interested in making the steelwork and in inserting this floating plane which carries the services. This reappears in other projects.

You also did IMMA, largely a symmetrical project, but here the detailing has stepped up a gear from the Point Depot.

That was an amazing project to be asked to do. I was dealing with a more momentous context – the Royal Hospital Kilmainham, a 17th-century building with all of its resonances. But there again you couldn't step away from the symmetry of that indisputable building. Making the new entrance hall directly opposite the projection of the Great Hall was the right thing to do, but within that you get a staircase that is asymmetrical, and heads off in one direction.

I was trying to create something which would make a point but which wouldn't date. That's debatable, I suppose. Some might say that all that glass and steel will date. But it wasn't a frivolous intervention; it was done in a serious way.

I suppose the formal moves are the most serious aspect, while that kind of technological steel language is a parallel consideration running through the work.

On the technical thing, I remember at a meeting trying to argue for the 12-metre-span staircase, saying that it was worth the effort because it was an indication of the new use, that it should be quite different and exciting. If it had been a technological experiment for its own sake then the technology might have been better.

Agriculture House on Kildare Street is one of your favourite projects. It distills many of the qualities in your work in a neat way.

Again you get this insertion, but it is consciously weighted in terms of one end which is exposed and one which isn't, and the two act as a counterpoint to each other. It is also about movement, yet it's not about a centre point. I took it on as a fascinating site – a double-height space where the internal linings were the same precast concrete as the exterior. You had this cavern, which at the same time had an amazing presence on the street. Conceptually we thought of it as an exterior space, an extension of the street, in which you stand these elements. I heard that a Japanese architect came to see it recently and he thought it was very John Hejduk, and that's probably correct!

But I suppose the repertoire changes. From being a student and interested in Corb's work, there was then an effort made not to be neo-Corbusian, even in an aesthetic way. In Swan Place there was an effort not to be connected linguistically to his work, to achieve a simplicity.

People have used words such as 'tact' and 'restraint' to describe your work, and certainly the simplicity translates across different languages.

One goal is to try to achieve a kind of inevitability about the work – that it will sit there for a long time and not become irrelevant. It's a very intangible thing to describe. Whenever I think I'm being really wild, somebody comes along and goes 'Oh, that's very restrained...' Well, you bring your baggage to the thing in one way, but underlying the work there has to be the idea that it's of sufficient quality to last.

I'm interested in an elemental approach to things, where a programme suggests that there are points of intensity, and that those points might find an architectural description. How you marry the particular form you choose to the particular programme can seem arbitrary at times, and it's hard to rationalise. But still the aim in a lot of projects, in the analysis of the pro-

Irish Museum of Modern Art, Royal Hospital Kilmainham, Dublin (1990-91)

Extension to National Gallery of Ireland, competition entry (1996)

gramme, is to get a kind of hierarchy established where one thing is the most important space and it might have this kind of expression, and another is secondary and it might act as a backdrop.

So why does the elevated meeting room seem so attractive? Is it because it is such an honest and simple form?

I think a similar thing is happening in a number of projects, like the National Gallery competition entry with the Jack Yeats Room that you walk underneath, and the education centre in Navan with the seminar room as a raised cube that you walk underneath. The reading of the project is that there's something important happening in that space, and that you experience it as a presence before you experience it as a space or volume.

The mention of presence reminds me of Luís Barragan saying: 'All architecture that does not express serenity is not fulfilling its spiritual purpose.'

That sounds wonderful. That's what we're trying to do! I suppose part of the conversation I'm having with myself at the moment is that certain projects will achieve that kind of differentiation through materials, that one element is made of a certain material, etc, and I tend not to do that. Up to now, at any rate, it's been more about the form of the thing, although I'm interested in moving away from the 'What's it made of? It's made of white' kind of critique.

The other thing that distinguishes your theatre of elements is the approach to scale. Often scale is a much more powerful tool in picking out elements than material. Is there a need to achieve a certain scale before an element might have the presence you are looking for?

Well, yes. The National Gallery broke all the conventions in that location by stepping out over the street. But our argument was that for a significant public building you could step out over the street – like the GPO [General Post Office], say – and people could walk underneath. We did a drawing for the competition, by accident almost, of the elevation of the original building on

Merrion Square. It turned out to be dimensionally identical to the Clare Street elevation in terms of height and frontage. So we had this drawing which was saying that the historical elevation was closed – the traditional idea of a museum, entering through a stone wall – and then on the new frontage we pushed things out to the street – the Jack Yeats Room, public places like the bookshop, the art library and restaurant. In an extraordinary way you would have this institution with two different frontages: one onto a space and one onto a street, each representing different times, different ideas about the nature of the same institution.

If Kildare Street is informed by movement, and the Blackrock Education Centre even more so, then the National Gallery and Walsall Gallery entries or Cork County Hall are more static.

Yes, they are. Cork County Hall, for example, is read more as one experience, whereas Blackrock unfolds more. Blackrock was also about going from public to private, and making a place which was separate. We really had to struggle to build within budget. The tendency with these buildings is that you make as simple a form as possible because of cost, but we went all out to make this arrangement, which is overstated in a way. There are all these individual elements joined by horizontal circulation, small-scale in terms of height. It was an experiment.

You say overstated, but in fact a lot of it is understated. Its success might lie in the clarity of the forms.

Well, in Blackrock the forms were very familiar, but you could easily imagine making that project with forms that were not so familiar if you had the time to investigate the qualities of each space more carefully.

They're familiar to you in that they're part of your repertoire.

Yes they are, but they also remind me of farm buildings in the Irish countryside.

Is that a conscious regionalism in your work?

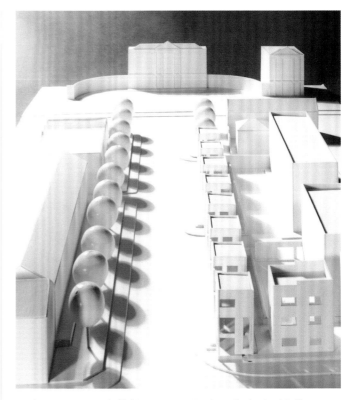

Housing at Queen Street / Blackhall Street, Dublin (1995-2002)

Housing at Glandore Road, Dublin (1998-2002)

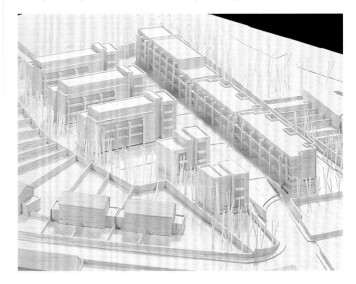

More subconscious. The office building we did in Laois is almost like a farm building that coalesced more. It wasn't so random, but it had all of these familiar bits, and is quite successful.

But how do you recreate that kind of familiarity in the new urban situation? I'm drawn to a comparison between your early housing at Chapelizod and Making a Modern Street*, which was a kind of Dublin Wiesenhof seventy years on – a collection of individually distinct narrow-fronted houses.*

I think people like to live in a terrace which uses repetition. It has a wonderful anonymity, and that's part of our received notion about the urban landscape. That's why you have to look at Modern Street as an exhibition, not a project, because it wasn't about everything being different. Chapelizod was about the site – an extraordinary physical landscape backing onto the Phoenix Park, the topography so astounding. The idea for it was a large aqueduct-like structure with a repetition of piers on the front. Frank Hall and I thought about it as a large-scale object in the landscape.

This repetition recurs in some of the more recent housing work, like Queen Street and Glandore Road.

The existing 1970s five-storey blocks on Queen Street are an interesting model. They have a flat on the ground floor and two duplexes stacked up with access decks. This narrow-frontage unit is a very interesting type which appears all over the city. So the task is to try to ensure that the new is not a critique of the old, which it would be if you were to make a deliberately domestic-scale intervention. We hope that it will be seen as an assembled scheme, that it has an old and a new part. And yet the concept of 'house', as a small group of apartments, is there in Queen Street, as it is in the Modern Street. Chapelizod was about a large-scale object in the landscape, but Queen Street is more about remaking the fabric of the street.

Glandore Road is quite a dense scheme. It is in a back-lands site with a very narrow entrance, so it is about making a garden space with a lot of fairly large buildings around it. Glandore is about making a place, Chapelizod is an object, and Queen Street is somewhere in-between.

The Modern Street attempted to establish a contemporary typology for urban living. But is it really more about rediscovering typological solutions?

Yes, the diversity wasn't necessarily a model. They were placed together in a shop-window and you could pick the one you liked, but they were related by a common theme which said you could put together five or six units in an urban 'house' with one common access, which was obviously a working model for living in the city. And Glandore Road is probably rather like a lot of 19th-century developments in London, which look onto common gardens. It's about having some common space that's not part of the public realm in the street-front sense.

Some of the devices used in your Modern Street house recur again in later work, such as the elevated courtyard.

Yes, I suppose in a way the elevated courtyard or space appears again in Arthouse and the Project. I was in the Unitarian Church on St Stephen's Green recently for the first time. I had never really looked at it before because it's sandwiched between two fairly nondescript office buildings, but you go in and you go up a staircase, and suddenly you're in this fabulous room, this special place, even though you're only four or five metres from the street. That's what I'm excited about in the Project Arts Centre, that we built this auditorium six metres above the street, which is an odd thing to do in one way. If you had a much bigger site you'd put it on the ground. But when you go in, the scale of the entrance, which is double-height, with the foyer above, still doesn't prepare you for the scale of the auditorium which is an enormous, hidden space.

Many of the cultural buildings of Temple Bar opt for this strategy of a hidden space allied to the façade-making part of their brief, including the Project.

I think so, yes. I hadn't been to the Project for a number of weeks, but I was there recently, and it's quite shocking in one way, because you're expecting a compression of everything, because on the drawing board it felt quite tight, and then sud-

continued on page 122

Irish Museum of Modern Art

Royal Hospital Kilmainham, Dublin 8
(1990-91)

This project involved adapting the east, west and south ranges of the historic 17th-century Royal Hospital at Kilmainham for the new Irish Museum of Modern Art. The north range, which houses the Great Hall, Master's quarters and chapel, was not part of the project.

The three ranges in question consist of repetitive rooms at each level, individually accessed by colonnades at ground floor and by corridors at upper levels. There are staircases in the corners of the plan, which, because of their hidden position, have no public presence. A new entrance hall was therefore located in the centre of the south range, axially related to the Great Hall in the north range, maintaining the inherent balance of the overall architectural composition. The new hall contains a steel and glass staircase in a double-height volume, and makes public the connection to the first floor where the main collections are housed.

The existing plan at first floor consisted of repetitive rooms accessed by corridors. A central determinant of the plan is the

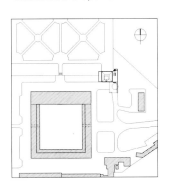

Section through the south range showing the double-height volume of the new entrance hall

Archive photographs of former grass courtyard and 1st floor corridor

Site plan showing Irish Museum of Modern Art, part of the Royal Hospital Kilmainham

opposite

The courtyard with new rolled-gravel surface and stone markings

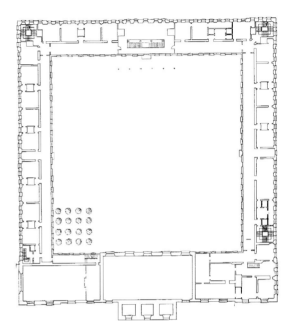

IRISH MUSEUM OF MODERN ART   Plans (ground, 1st floor)

Archway with pivot door to foyer   opposite
and courtyard beyond   View along south colonnade

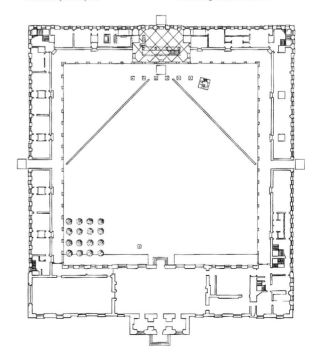

presence between each pair of rooms of a massive chimney stack. A new entry point to pairs of rooms is created opposite each of these stacks, thereby freeing the adjacent wall space for exhibition purposes. These first-floor rooms, combined with what were corridors but are now long galleries, were ideally suited to the new use with only minor modification.

The courtyard was changed from grass to a rolled-gravel surface, with stone markings indicating the new entrance hall. It is now the first 'room' of the museum, to be used for sculpture, installations, performance or special events. This precise and urbane treatment of the space now properly contrasts with the natural landscape of the overall site. It shows the colonnaded perimeter to the best advantage and has the intensity of an urban space.

The project, in its overall concept, takes nearly all its clues from the existing building, and pays due deference to it both formally and structurally. Aesthetically it proposes a clear distinction between old and new.

The new entrance hall with its 12m span steel and glass staircase

opposite

View of new staircase and entrance hall from 1st floor level

IRISH MUSEUM OF MODERN ART

Part of the inaugural exhibition, *Inheritance and Transformation*, 1991

Magdalena Jetelová, *Domestication of a Pyramid*, 1991

Antony Gormley, *Field*, 1995

opposite

Richard Deacon, *Kiss and Tell*, 1989

Arthouse

Multimedia Centre for the Arts,
Temple Bar, Dublin 2 (1992-95)

Arthouse is a four-storey-over-basement building incorporating a 19th-century house on Eustace Street. It houses the first Irish multimedia exhibition space, with full recording facilities and production unit at basement level, a large exhibition area at ground floor, and a library and networked information resources facility at first floor. At second-floor level there are a number of large seminar rooms and training suites, while at the uppermost level there are rentable offices, further administration space, and a conference/board room.

In urban design terms, the project forms one side of Curved Street, part of the Temple Bar Framework Plan by Group 91 Architects, of which this practice was a constituent member. The new street bisects the city block that stretched from Dame Street to Temple Bar, and with Meeting House and Temple Bar squares, creates a new east-west route stretching from

---

Views of model showing Eustace Street and Curved Street elevations

Site plan showing new Curved Street formed by Arthouse and the Music Centre

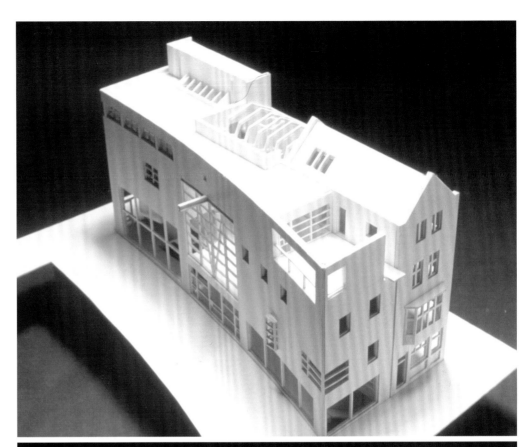

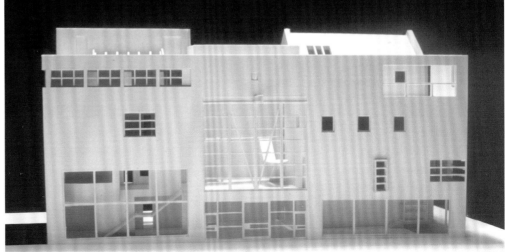

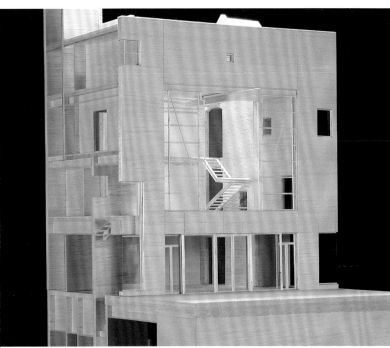

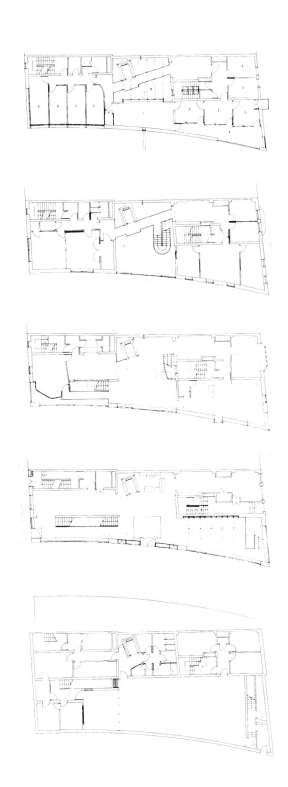

ARTHOUSE

Looking east towards Temple Lane, with the
Music Centre on the left

Cross-section through atrium

opposite

Cutaway model showing raised atrium

Looking west towards Eustace Street

Plans (basement, ground, 1st, 2nd, 3rd
floors)

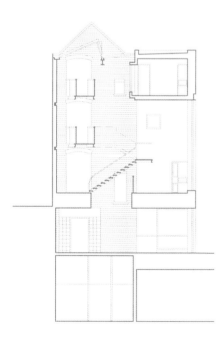

35

Essex Street to Crown Alley. Arthouse forms the south side of Curved Street, with the Temple Bar Music Centre forming the north side.

The Arthouse building has a transparent centre – corresponding to the void of the city block – allowing south light to reach the street. This central space – a raised, top-lit atrium – becomes the social focus of the building. Its glazed façade can be opened onto the street for special events or performances. It is accessed by a cascading staircase or by lift from reception at ground floor, and is crossed by open bridges which connect the upper levels.

In architectural terms, the project is a volumetrically connected series of spaces from basement to third floor. The main façade, with its formally powerful concave shape, provides the context for a series of highly specific openings, ranging in scale from the large moving screen of the atrium, to smaller, more specific fenestration in individual rooms.

Double-height glazed façade which can be opened onto the street

3rd floor bridge and conference room / boardroom

Basement multi-purpose space (photographed during *Vacationland* group exhibition, 2001)

opposite

View from raised court towards Curved Street

Walsall Art Gallery

England (1995)

International competition finalist

This competition was for a new art gallery in Walsall to house the permanent Garman Ryan Collection, and provide a variety of interactive exhibition and studio spaces, artists' studios, a conference suite, restaurant, and other retail uses. The project's aims were:

- to arrive at an elaborate and multi-layered architectural form from the richness of the programme
- to create a civic space for the town, extending its public realm
- to provide a unique place and identity for the Garman Ryan collection
- to propose a new facility which would invite the public to participate in all aspects of artistic endeavour and production.

The proposal makes a new courtyard space, contained by the gallery on three sides and by the canal basin to the west. This is seen as the major 'room' of the gallery, and will be highly visible from the street or from the canal basin. It can be used for a large range of activities, including performance, installation, sculpture and recreation. The foyer – the main introductory space to the gallery – is conceived of as being visually open, interactive and accessible.

The Garman Ryan Collection is located in its own special building. In urban design terms this building is seen as a special object which will be visible from other parts of the town, having the potential to become a symbol for both the collection and the gallery.

This project was shortlisted for the second stage of the competition.

View of courtyard formed by gallery on three sides and canal on fourth

Main façade

opposite

Rotating views of wood and perspex model

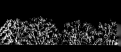

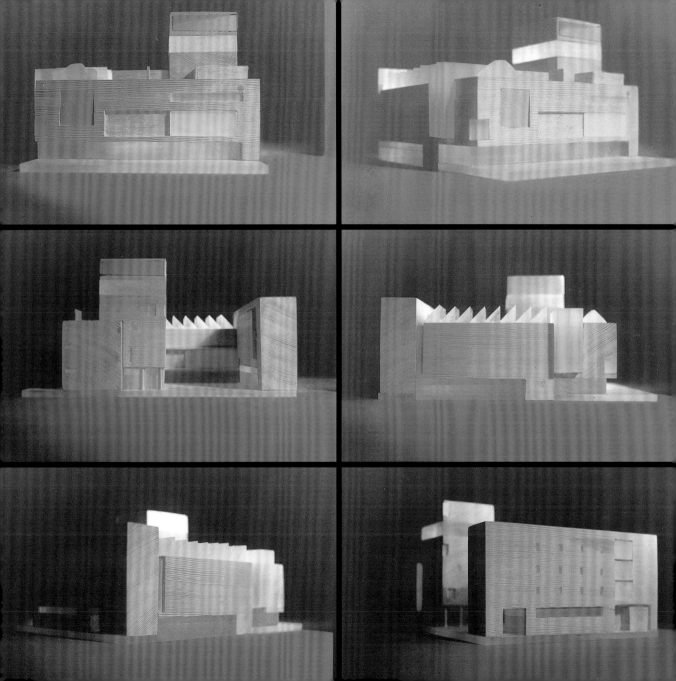

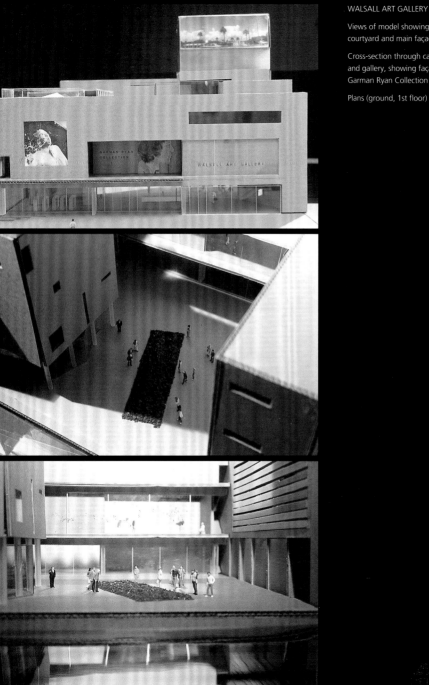

WALSALL ART GALLERY

Views of model showing canalside courtyard and main façade

Cross-section through canal, courtyard and gallery, showing façade of the Garman Ryan Collection building

Plans (ground, 1st floor)

WALSALL ART GALLERY

Views of model showing first-floor gallery overlooking courtyard, and day and night-time views of the courtyard

Plans (2nd, 3rd floors)

Cross-section

New Galleries, Irish Museum of Modern Art

Royal Hospital Kilmainham, Dublin 8
(1995-99)

This project was the conversion of the 18th-century Deputy Master's House at the Royal Hospital Kilmainham from former residential use into a highly serviced gallery which would comply with international lending criteria. The building will be used to house both travelling exhibitions and the expanding permanent collection of the Irish Museum of Modern Art. The project involved the refurbishment, conversion and extension of the existing building.

A new entrance courtyard, contained by a polished stone wall, is created to the east of the building, and can be accessed by steps or ramp. It directs people towards the new entrance, and onwards to the recently refurbished formal gardens to the north, while shielding the existing boiler house to the east from view. A large tree forms a natural canopy at the point of access to the new courtyard.

─────

Site plan showing Irish Museum of Modern Art with the New Galleries to the north

Views of model showing basement gallery and stepped gardens

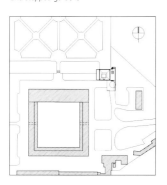

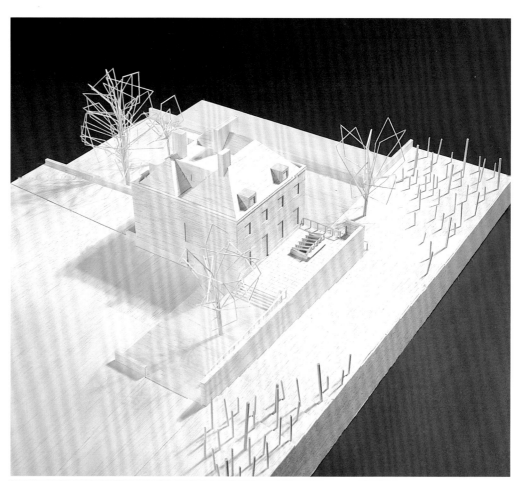

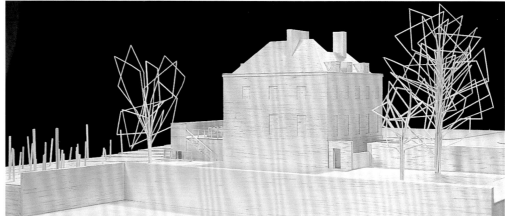

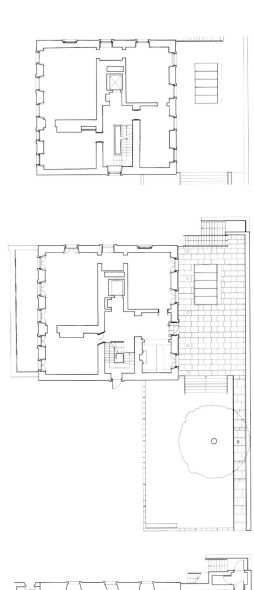

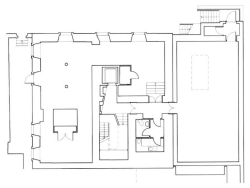

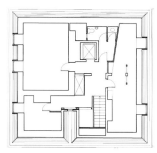

NEW GALLERIES, IMMA

Polished stone wall leading to New Galleries

2nd floor plan

opposite

View to formal gardens

New courtyard with sliding rooflight to
basement gallery

Plans (basement, ground, 1st floor)

NEW GALLERIES, IMMA

Existing room as gallery space

New underground gallery

Cross-section showing 'floating planes' for services in galleries

opposite (clockwise from top left)

'Floating plane'; perimeter circulation; entrance hall; 2nd floor archive space

A new exhibition space below the entrance court gives greater flexibility as it is larger than those available in the house. The main gallery spaces in the existing building are at ground and first-floor level, while the second floor is for administrative and archival uses. Circulation on the gallery floors is primarily along the perimeter of the building, releasing the inner walls for hanging purposes.

The introduction of air conditioning into this old structure was accommodated by inserting a 'floating plane' in each of the main rooms. This plane houses all of the necessary ductwork and lighting.

A proposed sculpture court on the north side of the building will become another event on a route through the grounds of the Royal Hospital, from the main building, through the new court, and onwards to the formal gardens.

The restoration of the external fabric of the building was overseen by the Office of Public Works.

Extension to National Gallery of Ireland

Clare Street, Dublin 2 (1996)
international competition finalist

In an international competition, ten firms were invited to make proposals for a 5,000m² extension to the National Gallery of Ireland.

The aim of this proposal was to make a new wing which would act cohesively with the existing building and provide the required accommodation in a manner that would enhance the experience of the overall building, while creating, in overall terms, a modern gallery for the 21st century.

The site for the extension on Clare Street is at a pivotal point in the city, forming a junction between the Georgian precinct and the rest of the city centre. The proposal recognises and reinforces this set of circumstances.

The new entrance portico – a stone and glass cube elevated six metres above the street – signals the presence of the gallery from Clare Street and Merrion Square to the east, and South Leinster Street to the west, creating a punctuation mark between two sets of circumstances. It extends over the pavement in a contemporary interpretation of a traditional architectural device seen elsewhere in Dublin, most notably at the GPO on O'Connell Street and at the Bank of Ireland (formerly the House of Parliament) at College Green.

The other element in the composition is a curved, four-storey, glazed façade, which continues the building line of South Leinster Street and makes the context for arrival and entry under the cube.

The gallery spaces are located on the upper levels, which correspond to the ground and first-floor levels within the existing building. Ancillary functions are located below these levels, with the more public uses positioned on Clare Street, creating a visually open and interactive relationship with the city.

Site plan showing existing gallery on Merrion Square and new extension on Clare Street

Axonometric of architectural elements

opposite

View of the entrance portico on Clare Street

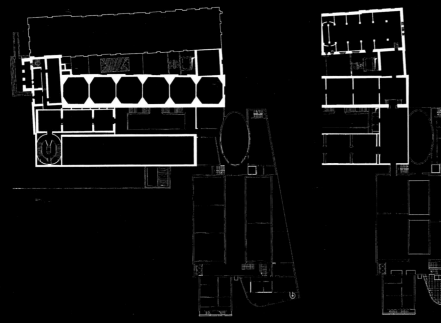

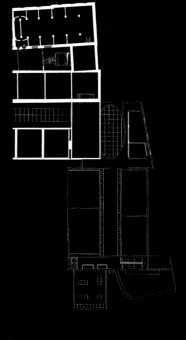

EXTENSION TO NATIONAL GALLERY

Plans of existing gallery and new extension
(ground, mezzanine, 1st floor (bottom))

Plans of existing gallery and new extension
(2nd, 3rd, 4th floors (top))

opposite

View of the entrance portico and curved,
glazed façade on Clare Street

Sections through new galleries

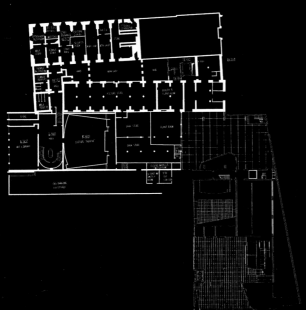

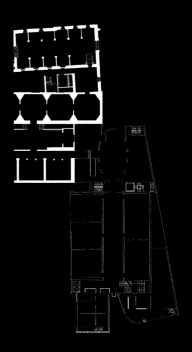

Project Arts Centre
Temple Bar, Dublin 2 (1996-2000)

The Project Arts Centre, established in 1966, was the first arts centre in Ireland. Thirty years later it had outgrown its original premises, which was a dilapidated, predominantly single-storey industrial structure at the heart of Temple Bar. The new building is a purpose-built facility on the same highly restricted site.

The brief required the provision of a multipurpose performance space which would seat up to 250 people in a variety of configurations, a smaller complementary space for up to 100 people, and a dedicated visual arts space, together with all of the necessary support functions of foyer and box office, administrative offices, dressing rooms, control rooms and storage.

Because of the highly restricted nature of the site, a fundamental decision was made to locate the main auditorium at first-floor level. This primary strategy led to a number of architectural decisions which determined the formal arrangement of the overall scheme. The volume of the main auditorium is set back from the building line by five metres,

The façade of the new Project Arts Centre on East Essex Street

The former Project building

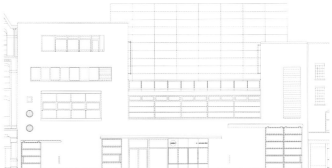

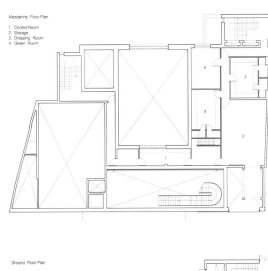

Mezzanine Floor Plan

1. Control Room
2. Storage
3. Dressing Room
4. Green Room

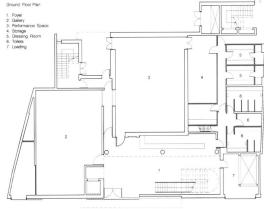

Ground Floor Plan

1. Foyer
2. Gallery
3. Performance Space
4. Storage
5. Dressing Room
6. Toilets
7. Loading

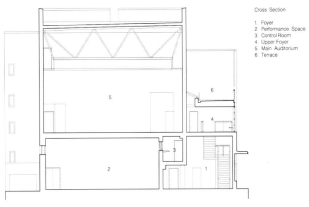

Cross Section

1. Foyer
2. Performance Space
3. Control Room
4. Upper Foyer
5. Main Auditorium
6. Terrace

PROJECT ARTS CENTRE

Cutaway model and cross-section showing performance space and first-floor auditorium behind double-height foyer

Site plan and plans (ground, mezzanine)

opposite

Plans (1st, 2nd, 3rd floors)

Part-model of façade

Long section through foyer (with steel-clad auditorium behind)

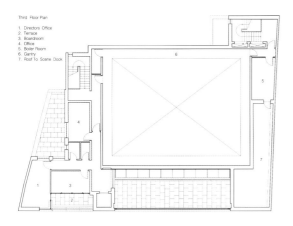

Third Floor Plan

1. Directors Office
2. Terrace
3. Boardroom
4. Office
5. Boiler Room
6. Gantry
7. Roof To Scene Dock

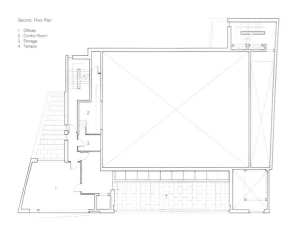

Second Floor Plan

1. Offices
2. Control Room
3. Storage
4. Terrace

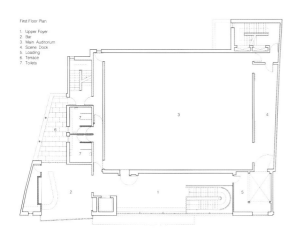

First Floor Plan

1. Upper Foyer
2. Bar
3. Main Auditorium
4. Scene Dock
5. Loading
6. Terrace
7. Toilets

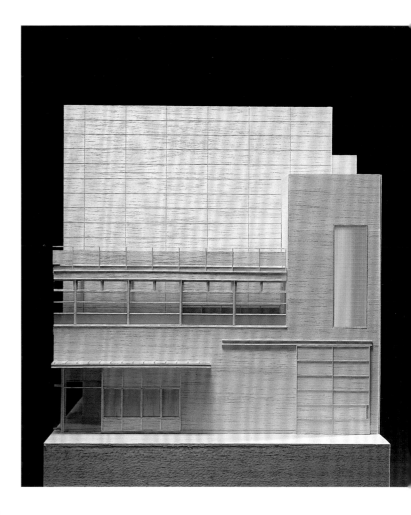

Cross Section

1. Foyer
2. Gallery
3. Loading Bay
4. Upper Foyer
5. Bar
6. Offices
7. Terrace
8. Directors Office
9. Boardroom

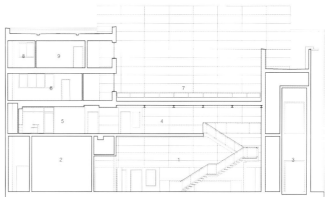

installation/multimedia work, theatre, dance and music.

In formal terms the building is a response to a complex series of urban conditions and necessities. It presents a relatively closed elevation to the street, which was a strong characteristic of the original Project building. It invites investigation rather than presenting a 'shop window'. Formal and service elements of the building coexist on the front façade, which is a product of the urban condition and which is expressed through the use of large sliding doors of varying sizes, depending on their use. The performance space is clad in galvanised steel sheets, seen from the foyer as one enters. The rest of the building is plastered and painted an electric blue to further distinguish its public function from the general context.

Entrance foyer

Looking east along East Essex Street

opposite

Upper foyer leading to main auditorium

allowing sunlight to reach the street.

The main performance space is flanked by two 'bookends' of accommodation, the eastern one containing the gallery at ground floor, the bar at first floor, and administration over. The western flank provides space for a large goods lift serving the scene dock at first floor. They both relate to the scale of adjoining properties.

The entrance foyer is a long, narrow, double-height space containing box office, reception and the main staircase leading to the upper foyer. It also provides access to the gallery and the smaller auditorium. The upper foyer is a low horizontal space, fully glazed to the street and roof-lit at its rear to reveal the wall of the performance space. The bar is an extension of this area. The performance space is accessed through an 'extended' doorway from the upper foyer. The abrupt change in scale between both foyers (which are, respectively, narrow and vertical and low and horizontal) and the large volume that one encounters is dramatic and unexpected.

The main spaces are consciously less functionally specific than traditional theatre spaces. They can be used for a range of activities, including

PROJECT ARTS CENTRE

Day and night-time views of the main entrance on East Essex Street

Detail section, elevation and plan of entrance canopy and sliding screen

PROJECT ARTS CENTRE

Entrance foyer, with staircase leading to
upper foyer and main auditorium

Roof terrace formed by 5m set-back of
main auditorium from building line

Detail of main staircase

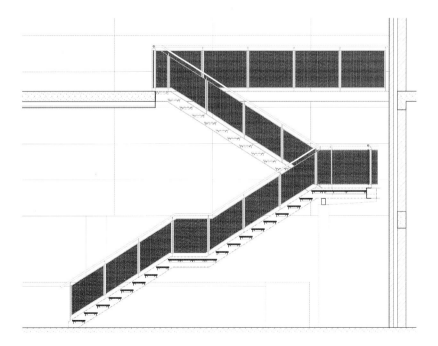

PROJECT ARTS CENTRE

Main auditorium (photographed during the opening exhibition, *Somewhere Near Vada*, curated by Jaki Irvine, 2000)

End-on theatre configuration

opposite

Main auditorium / performance space

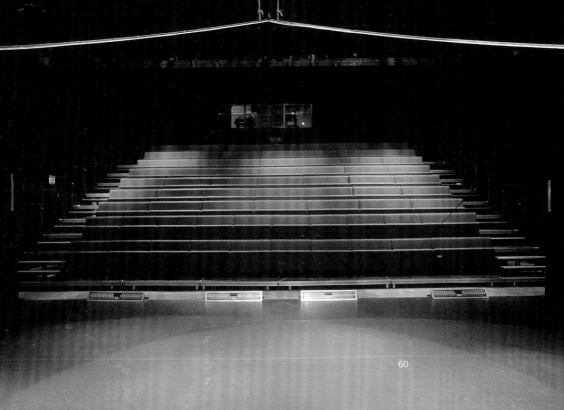

Meeting and Conference Facilities, Dept of Agriculture
Kildare Street, Dublin 2 (1993-94)

The brief was to provide a new reception and waiting area, additional meeting rooms, and upgraded security provisions for the Dept of Agriculture. The context for the project was the existing double-height entrance hall in its Kildare Street headquarters – a speculatively built mid-1970s office building.

The proposal treats the hall as a quasi-public/outdoor space, into which are placed a series of planes and objects which use the rear wall of the hall as a backdrop. A gallery at first-floor level accommodates the two meeting rooms and conference room. They are accessed by a new stone and steel staircase at one end of the hall, or by a new connection into the existing lift lobby. The stairs, with its spine wall and canopy, acts as a formal counterpoint to the distorted elliptical form of the conference room at the far end, adjacent to Kildare Place.

Night-time view of Agriculture House

Plans of foyer (ground, 1st floor)

opposite

Conference room from the street

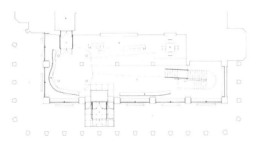 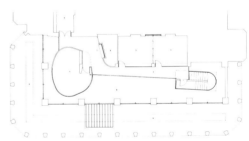

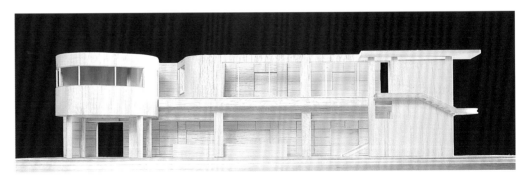

The project introduces a new glass lobby and canopy into the existing arcade, and this is washed with light. The reception desk is located in the low horizontal space beneath the new gallery. The large tapestry by Patrick Scott which was originally commissioned for the building is relocated, and is now seen in a fragmented way as one ascends the staircase.

DEPT OF AGRICULTURE

View of foyer and 1st floor gallery leading to elliptical conference room

The stairs with its spine wall and canopy

Axonometric of architectural insertions

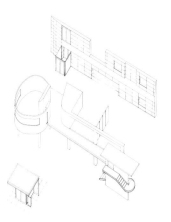

Office Building,
Dawson Street
Dublin 2 (1998-2002)

The commission from Dublin City Council was to provide a high-quality office building to be let on the open market. The site was a vacant lot adjacent to the Mansion House which had been used as a surface car park. It therefore constituted a break in the urban fabric, exposing the gables of the adjoining properties and the interior of the city block. A right of way had to be maintained to allow access to a multi-storey car park. The Mansion House itself is set back from the street, and establishes a rectangular forecourt onto Dawson Street, contained at its northern end by the Royal Irish Academy.

The new building has five floors of flexible office space over a basement car park. It is L-shaped in configuration, with the main volume of the building set back from the street, allowing a diagonal view of the Mansion House from the south.

Computer model of new building

Site plans – before and after

View to Dawson Street, with Royal Irish Academy and Mansion House

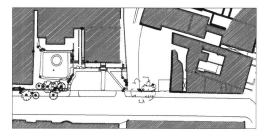

The general height of the building is five storeys, while the forward section on the street, is four floors. The flank of the building is three and four storeys where it addresses the Mansion House more directly. The fenestration at this point is in the form of a large glazed screen of opalescent, non-transparent glass to avoid direct overlooking of the formal dining room.

The set-back volume of the building is clad in Jura limestone in deference to the general colour of the Mansion House precinct, while the forward element is clad in red sandstone to visually connect with the adjacent brick buildings on the street. The use of these contrasting materials reduces the overall visual mass of the building, while increasing the perception of depth of the site. The sandstone element is stack-bonded, and its glazing is either flush or forward of the wall plane. In contrast, the limestone is stretcher-bonded, and the punched openings have recessed glazing with aluminium liners to the reveals.

In general terms the building is a particular response in terms of scale, formal arrangement, architectural language and colour to a complex urban context on what is regarded as one of the finest streets in the city.

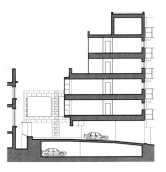

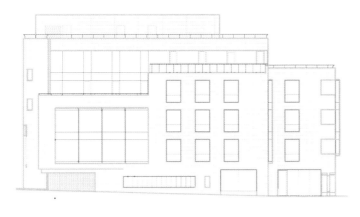

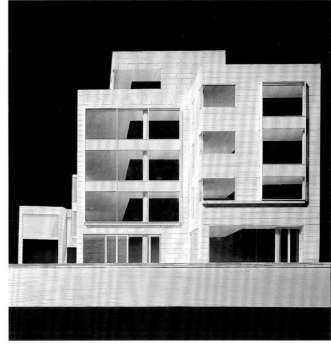

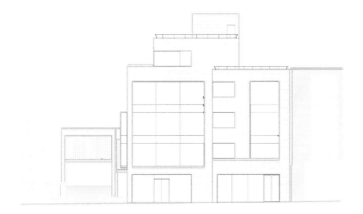

Mansion House and Dawson St elevations

Model view

Plans (ground, 1st, 3rd, 4th floors)

opposite

Views of model showing stepped profile of building in plan and section, and the two-storey 'light box' facing the Mansion House

Cross-section through building

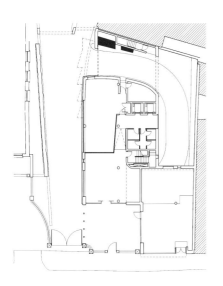

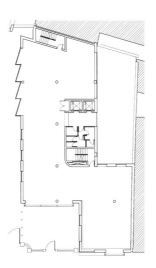

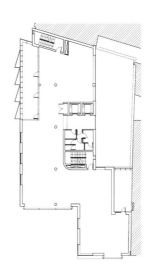

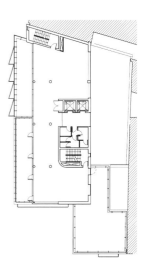

OFFICE BUILDING, DAWSON STREET

Views of the building as it nears
completion

68

Tower Building, Grand Canal Quay
Dublin 4 (1999-2002)

In this scheme, a disused, 19th-century canalside tower building is converted into a mini office block with small suites of offices on each floor. The building is tightly bound by Grand Canal Quay to the west, the Grand Canal to the east, the railway bridge to the north, and a small open area to the south.

The scheme involves the introduction of a freestanding glazed stair and lift tower to the south to serve the building. Aesthetically, a clear distinction is made between the loadbearing character of the existing brick tower and the more transparent lightweight contemporary elements of the core and penthouse. Together they form a complementary composition of old and new.

Views of model from north and east

Computer model showing stair tower and penthouse

Site plan

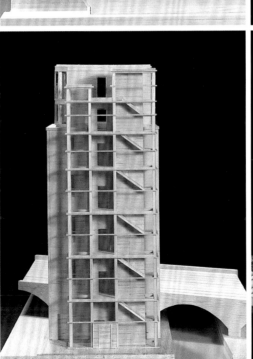

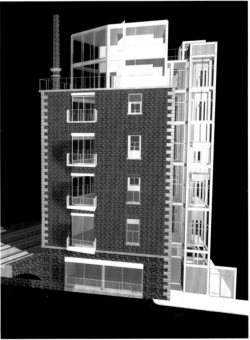

Tower Building under construction

Plans (ground, typical floor, lower and
upper penthouse floors)

opposite

View of completed Tower Building from
Grand Canal Harbour

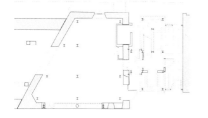   

Redevelopment & Extension to Cork County Hall
Victoria Cross, Cork (1999-)
international competition winner

County Hall, the administrative headquarters for County Cork, was built in the 1960s. This project for its redevelopment involves the recladding and general fitting out of the existing tower block, along with the provision of further office accommodation in a six-storey extension, and a new concourse and council chamber.

The scheme proposes an L-shaped arrangement of tower block and extension, embracing a triple-height concourse containing the council chamber as a special element. This primary strategy brings County Hall into a direct relationship with the street.

The concourse is seen as mediating between the various elements of the composition. It is a rectilinear hall of

---

View of the refurbished County Hall from the Lee Fields (to the west)

Before and after views from Victoria Cross (to the east)

opposite

Computer model of competition stage

CORK COUNTY HALL

View of model from north, showing new six-storey office extension, with the triple-height concourse and council chamber in the foreground, adjoining the re-clad 1960s tower block

North elevation

Plans (ground, 1st 2nd, 3rd floors)

opposite

View of model showing new six-storey office extension, with the triple-height concourse and council chamber in the foreground

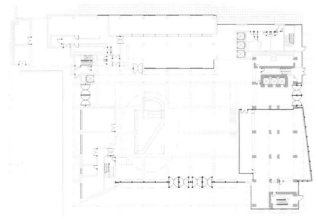

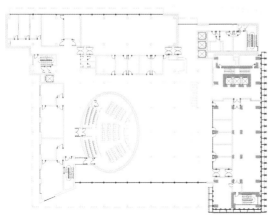

overleaf

Computer model of project at planning stage showing new concourse and re-clad tower, and entrance with ovoid council chamber on the left

Cross-section through new office extension and concourse

Section through council chamber and tower block

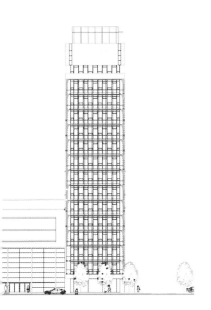

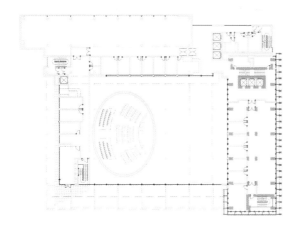

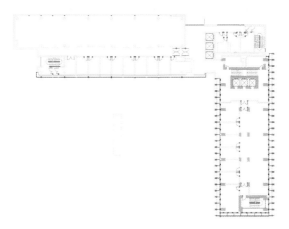

steel columns supporting a slender roof. It sits in the L-shaped configuration established by the tower block and the new extension, and contains all of the more public functions at ground, first and second-floor levels. The concourse can be accessed from three sides, allowing easy movement to the building from the various car-parking areas.

The extension forms the southern flank of the proposed complex. It is six storeys high, and accommodates public counters and meeting rooms at ground floor, the members' rooms and chairman's office at first floor, and back-up administration office space on the remaining floors. Its southern side is treated elementally with set-backs at ground and fifth floor.

The existing building has many strong characteristics which the proposal enhances and highlights. Its relationship to the main road is powerful and elegant, presenting a slender, delicately proportioned form on approach. The additions, both in terms of scale and disposition, are arranged to avoid compromising its form. Its general aesthetic of a layered façade – comprising applied, non-structural frame, and set back, full-height glazing – is endorsed and reinterpreted by the proposal.

A new outer façade consists of primary vertical mullions which span from floor perimeter to floor perimeter in line with the existing structural column grid. Secondary mullions support a system of glass louvres which are climactically controlled. This active façade will allow a naturally ventilated, high-quality working environment, even in the context of a high-rise building.

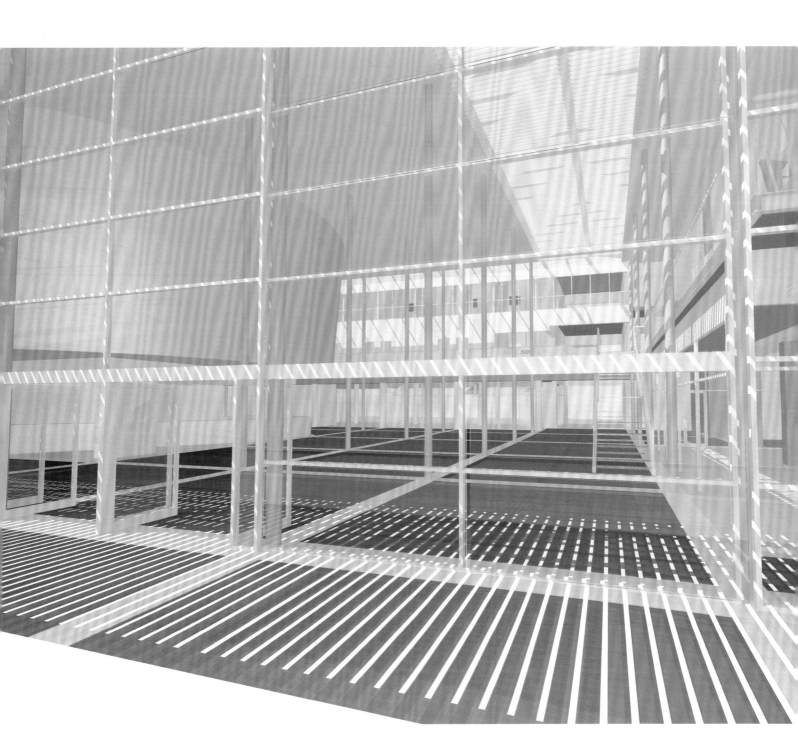

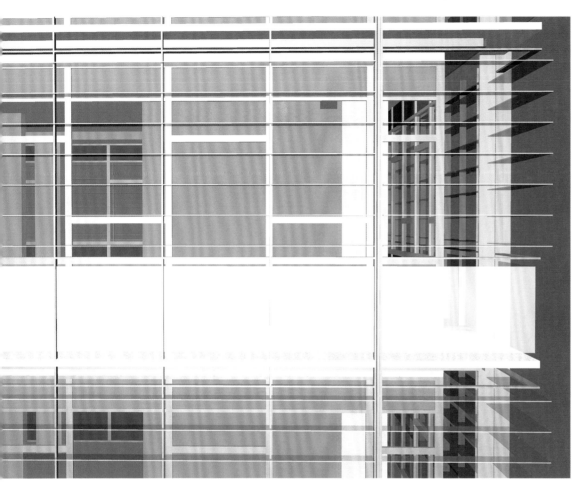

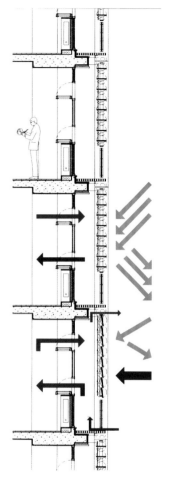

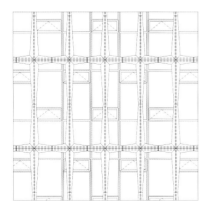

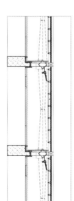

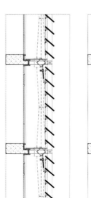

CORK COUNTY HALL

Details of the re-clad façade showing existing cruciform overlaid with louvre support structure, and active façade in different modes

Section and elevation – competition stage

opposite

Computer model of competition submission showing proposed layered façade

Blackrock Education Centre
Dun Laoghaire, Co Dublin (1994-96)

This was the first purpose-built in-service training building for teachers to be commissioned by the Dept of Education & Science. The project creates a private inner courtyard, around which are grouped the various elements of the programme. Entry to the building is via a smaller outer courtyard which establishes the transition from the campus to the more private world of the centre.

The first and most open part of the entrance hall is addressed by the elliptical seminar room, the library, and the administration and director's office suite. Leading off the foyer is a linear circulation/meeting area which looks onto the courtyard. It also serves the group rooms, which can be interconnected in a variety of combinations. The library, with its reading area, is also expressed as a special element. The final, most private side of the garden is formed by the research base which looks back towards the entrance foyer.

The courtyard is of rolled gravel, and is planted with specimen trees. It is a tranquil space, acting as a focus around which the elements are placed. Externally, the building appears as an amalgamation of various forms around a walled enclosure, with trees visible from the outside. The external finish is an off-white render, rather like the colour of Portland stone.

Views of model

Plan and site plan

opposite

Views of the complex, its entrance court and private internal courtyard

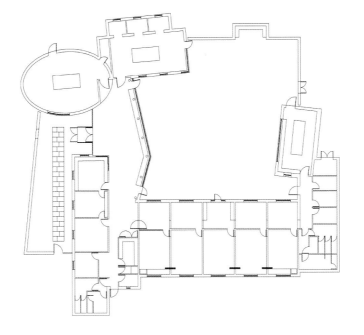

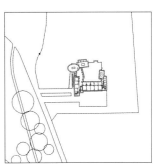

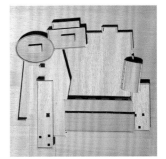

BLACKROCK EDUCATION CENTRE

View from south-east

Section through foyer, entrance elevation, and section through meeting rooms

Axonometric

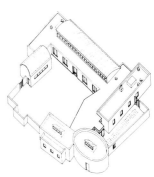

Navan Education Centre
Navan, Co Meath (1998-2000)

This building provides facilities for in-service training of teachers. It consists of a series of meeting rooms and a main seminar room, a state-of-the-art library/resource room, an IT training suite, and administration and general social areas. These various elements are expressed as individual volumes, joined by a glazed foyer and a two-storey linear circulation space. The most significant space is the main seminar room, which is expressed as a large volume over the main entrance, addressing the north-west corner of the site nearest the town. The foyer/social area – the first space which one enters – can be used for informal gatherings, and is glazed towards the existing stone perimeter wall.

The remaining accommodation is organised around a double-height, top-lit circulation space, with the larger rooms on the western side and the smaller spaces facing eastwards towards an earth bank. Parking is placed towards the northern boundary, and is surrounded by planting. A triangular lawn space is formed between the building and the earth bank. The building is finished in a smooth render.

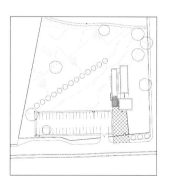

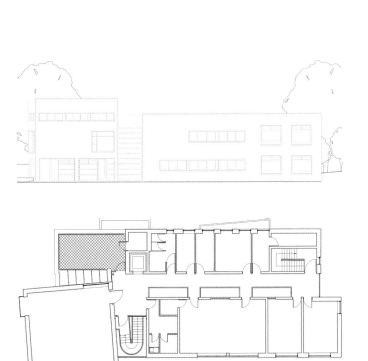

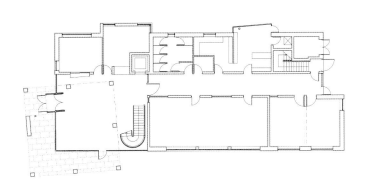

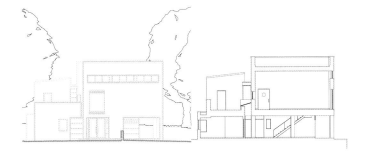

NAVAN EDUCATION CENTRE

Views of the building from the north and west show the individual volumes of the constituent elements

Cross-section and north elevation

opposite

Views of foyer and double-height, top-lit circulation space

East elevation

Plans (ground, 1st floor)

Main (south) elevation and cross-section

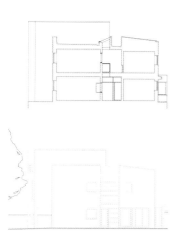

Laois Education Centre
Portlaoise, Co Laois (1996-98)

The accommodation provided comprises of meeting and seminar rooms, a library, a research base, administration and ancillary facilities.

In section the building is split-level, which differentiates between the functions of entrance, reception and administration on the lower level, and the more dedicated teaching and meeting areas on the upper. A major concern in the building was that all of the spaces would benefit from an abundance of daylight. This is achieved through the provision of rooflights, high-level glazing, and the careful positioning of windows to allow light to reflect off wall surfaces.

The building is located towards the higher part of the site to take advantage of views and orientation. Car-parking is accommodated to one side and enclosed by planting, with a further screen of planting to the south, adjacent to existing residential properties. The building is rendered and plastered in the tradition of many buildings in the Irish landscape.

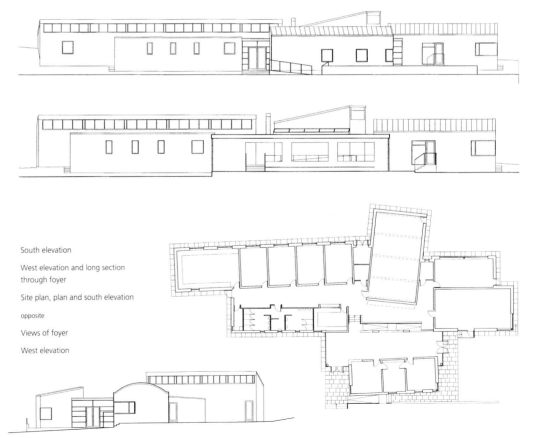

South elevation

West elevation and long section through foyer

Site plan, plan and south elevation

opposite

Views of foyer

West elevation

Science of Materials Building, Trinity College Dublin

invited competition (1995)

The competition involved making proposals for a new laboratory complex which could be built in various stages. It is located at the less developed eastern end of the historic campus.

This proposal created two new spaces for the college. The new spatial arrangement would establish a proper eastern gateway to Trinity College, and act as the modern counterpart to Front Gate.

The spaces take the form of two squares: one is the completion of the space between the botany and physics departments, the other a substantial new enclosure which, through its form and arrangement, integrates existing buildings, both new and historic, into a coherent whole. The new square takes the form of an inhabited plinth on which are placed a number of buildings, each of which has a specific role in the overall composition.

The ground floor of each building has a glazed foyer – a social gathering area looking onto the square. The sunken courtyard is seen as a further extension of that idea at the lower-plinth level. In terms of materials, the buildings are prismatic glazed objects placed on a stone plinth.

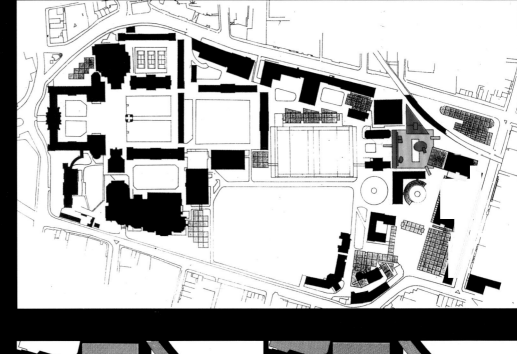

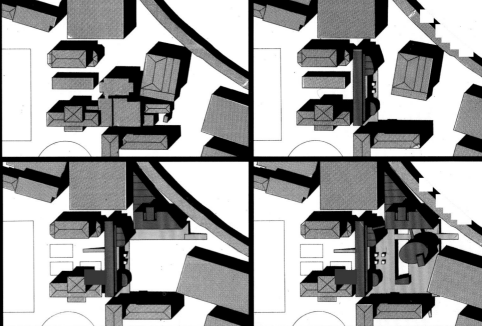

Plan of Trinity College, and site plans showing stages of development

opposite

Views of project

Sections through the new building

Plans (ground, 1st, 2nd floors)

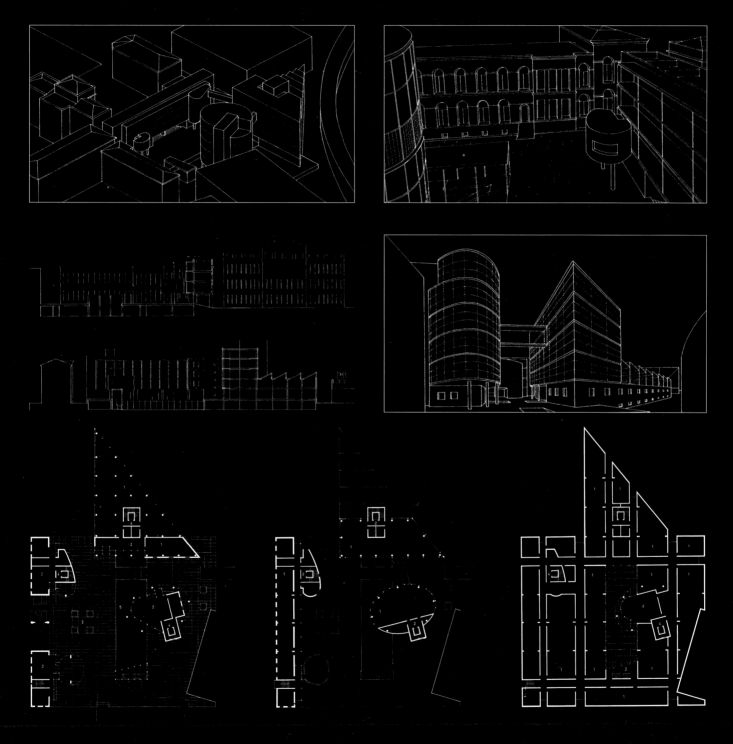

An tIonad Náisiúnta Oideachais Gaeilge

National Centre for Irish Language Education, Ballyvourney, Co Cork (2000-)

The site was originally part of the grounds of Coláiste Íosagán on the edge of Ballyvourney. It is surrounded by trees and is spatially like a large outdoor room. The scheme proposes that access is through the existing formal entrance to the overall property, leading to a driveway which follows the line of poplar trees to the parking area. This is located on the northern side of the site, and is contained by a wall of cypress trees and the proposed building.

The centre is a two-storey structure. Its northern side is wall-like in appearance, while its southern side is a framed structure with an oversailing roof which embraces a large outdoor veranda. The main seminar room is expressed as a distinct cubic volume in the configuration. The majority of the spaces to the south are fully glazed to establish a strong visual connection with the beautiful setting.

The building is entered from the car park through a large, double-height glazed screen leading to the foyer/social area, with adjacent reception and administration areas. A multi-purpose heritage/exhibition space adjoins the foyer and is open to the visiting public. The majority of the accommodation is organised linearly along a top-lit atrium to the west – IT room and offices at ground-floor level, and research bases at first-floor level. The main staircase is a freestanding element in the entrance hall, leading to an upper foyer. The main seminar room is located at first-floor level, and has a small

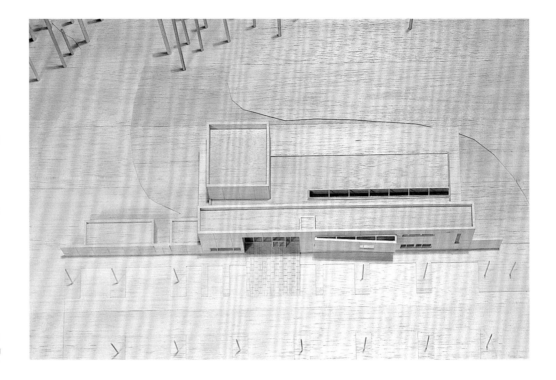

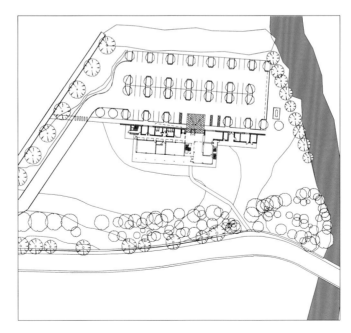

recording studio adjoining it. The remainder of this floor comprises a series of meeting rooms/research bases, with the boardroom/library expressed as a particular volume on the northern elevation.

The building is conceived of as a pavilion, and the materials reinforce that primary concept. It is clad in timber panels to create a sense of lightness.

Model and site plan

opposite

Views of model from north and south

Cross-sections through the building

Plans (ground, 1st floor)

90

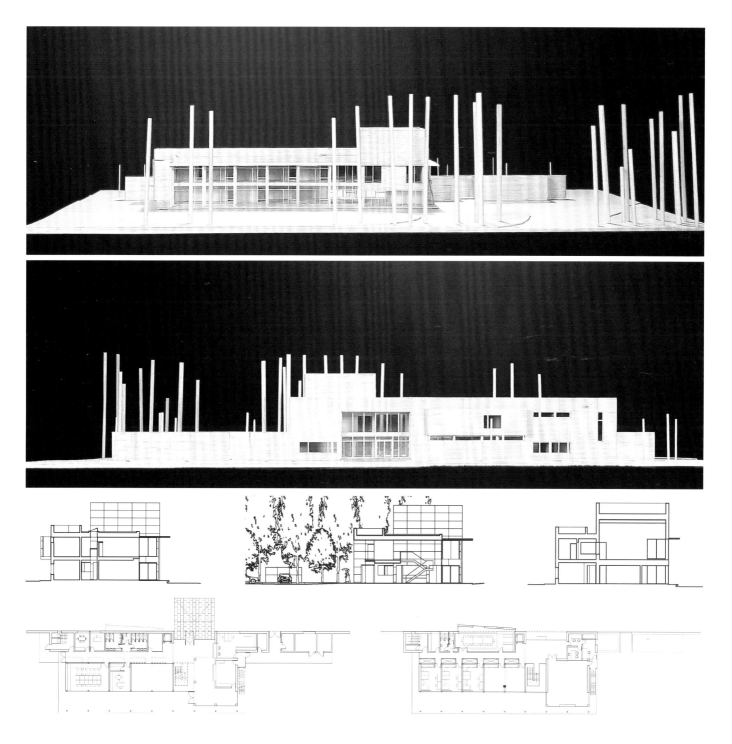

Making a Modern Street –
An Urban Proposal
Dublin (1991)

This project was part of a collaborative effort by Group 91 Architects, a consortium of eight practices with an interest in both architectural and urban design. Each practice was given a prescribed plot and asked to make a proposition about urban living.

This scheme was for a narrow-frontage plot. It comprised a commercial ground floor with five one-bedroom apartments above. The project was seen as an opportunity to experiment with small-scale, high-density urban living units and their aggregation.

The apartments are organised around a raised court at first floor, which is accessed via a cascading staircase from the street. The raised court acts as a lightwell for the scheme, and contains an eccentric steel staircase. This stairs leads to a bridge at second floor and to a shared south-facing roof terrace above, and is an important social element in the scheme where chance meetings and conversation can take place. Three of the apartments are horizontal in arrangement, and two are duplexes.

In spite of their small square footage they have a certain spatial generosity, being either open-plan or volumetrically arranged depending on unit type. The common roof terrace and access stair assume an intended importance and use because of the small dwelling size. The street façade is of brick, with steel, glass and concrete insertions. The elevations to the lightwell are of glass block. A steel and glass rooflight shelters the common stair.

The project was intended for construction but a developer was not found. If built it would have been a living exhibition describing a variety of options for urban living.

Cutaway axonometric showing the stairs leading to raised court and the roof terrace

Plans (ground, 1st, 2nd, 3rd floors)

opposite

Cutaway model of the project

Making a Modern Street – the combined proposals of the eight practices in Group 91

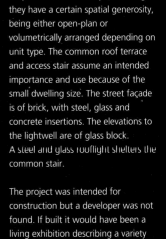
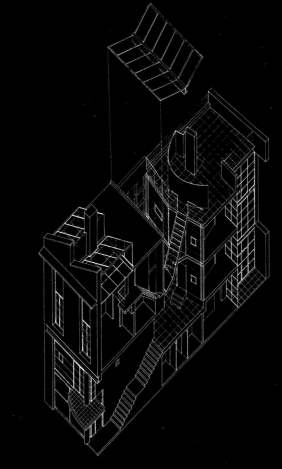

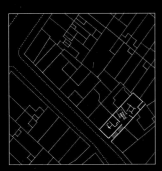

Queen Street Housing

Queen Street / Blackhall Street,
Dublin 1 (1995-2002)

This project for Dublin City Council
provides social housing by converting
a number of existing 1970s flats and
building new accommodation. The
existing context was a city block
which had four freestanding
apartment buildings. The urban block
and its edge had been destroyed
through demolition, and the project,
therefore, had the dual purpose of
providing the necessary
accommodation along with
reconstructing the city block in an
overall scheme.

The existing buildings are five storeys
and are a standard type built in many
parts of the city. They have a flat at
ground floor with two duplexes
stacked above, accessed by open
decks. They are generally an
amalgamation of a number of narrow
frontages of this arrangement.
Our proposal, given that the basic
architecture had a certain clarity, was
to extensively refurbish the existing
units, but to modify the means of
access by introducing a series of
staircases, each serving four dwellings
above, as a substitute for the open-
deck approach, which had not
worked well in social terms. The new
buildings in the scheme are three or

Views of existing blocks of flats on Queen
Street / Blackhall Street, and the Blue Coat
School on Blackhall Place

opposite

Models showing before and after views
down Blackhall Street

Model showing section through refurbished
block, new courtyard and new housing,

Part-model showing the new Blackhall
Street / Queen Street corner

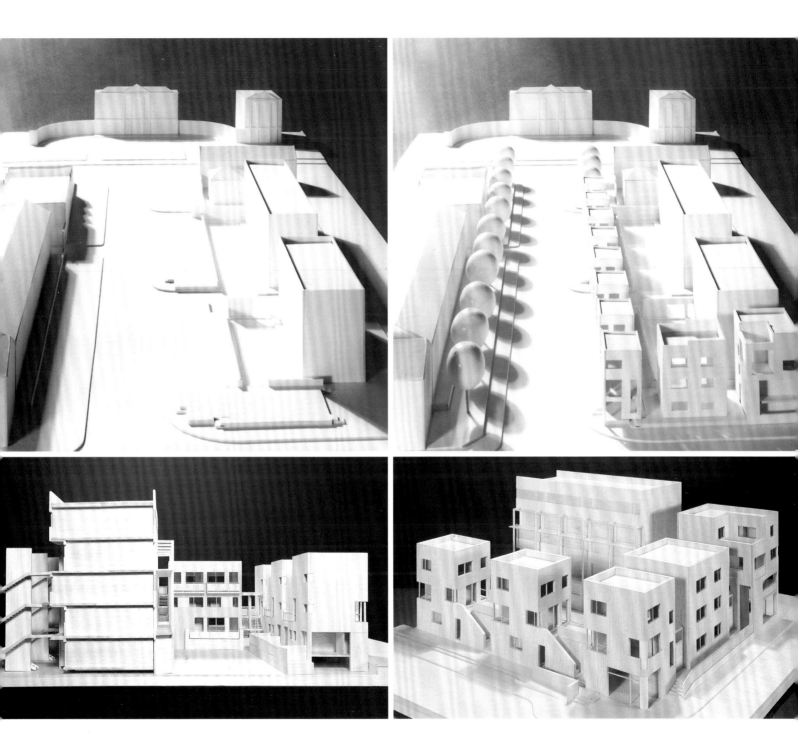

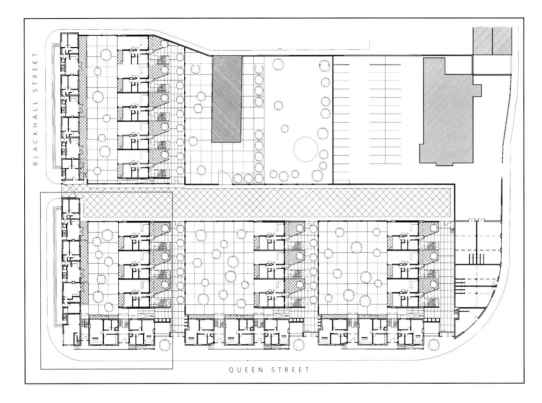

four storeys, and generally re-establish the street wall and street edge on three sides. On the southern side of the scheme a perforated terrace with a continuous ground floor, along with formal tree-planting opposite, creates a new street space which is axial with the Blue Coat School to the west. To the east, on Queen Street, a repetitive series of blocks of three and four storeys remakes the street, while at the north end a four-storey curved building completes the urban block. Generally, dwellings are arranged in small groups around common staircases, promoting a sense of ownership.

The overall plan will provide a structured arrangement of public, semi-public and private open space to replace the discrete environment in which the blocks currently sit. A number of pedestrian streets parallel to the existing buildings form the backbone of this new plan. Walled common gardens are contained between new and existing buildings, and are clearly defined as being in the ownership of a sub-grouping of dwellings. Most of the 120 dwellings are two-bed units, with a small number of larger three-bed apartments.

The scheme is seen as a careful amalgamation of new and existing elements into a coherent scheme, which will provide a new context for living in the area while repairing a damaged part of the city fabric.

Blackhall Street elevation (with refurbished blocks behind)

Site plan of development (with area of part-model outlined in colour)

Queen Street elevation

opposite

Aerial view of scheme under construction

Plans (ground, 1st, 2nd, 3rd floors)

Long section (with new blocks on street edges and 3 refurbished blocks at centre)

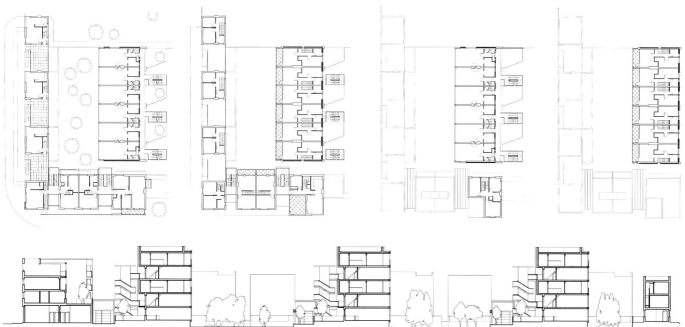

QUEEN STREET HOUSING

Views of living spaces in new housing

Typical access stair and perforated terrace

opposite

View down Blackhall Street to Blue Coat School as the south block nears completion (Summer 2002)

The first residents move in

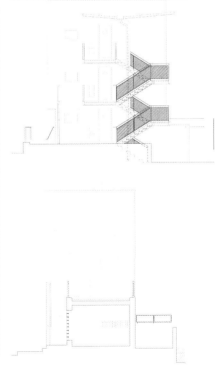

Apartment Development, Glandore Road
Dublin 9 (1998-2002)

The scheme proposes a high-density, low-rise development of apartments in blocks of varying heights and configurations, placed in a landscaped common garden.

A three and four-storey-high terrace of blocks is placed parallel to the eastern boundary. Bedrooms face east, and living spaces face west towards the common garden. At right angles to this arrangement are a series of blocks of varying lengths which step upwards from three to four storeys as they extend eastwards. The two shortest blocks are stepped from two to three storeys. This range of buildings is accessed on the northern side, and have large south-facing terraces. Generally, bedrooms face north and living rooms south.

A decision was made to place virtually all the parking below ground, thus

Views of model showing terrace of blocks on eastern boundary and the series of smaller south-facing blocks

Site plan

opposite

Computer model of scheme

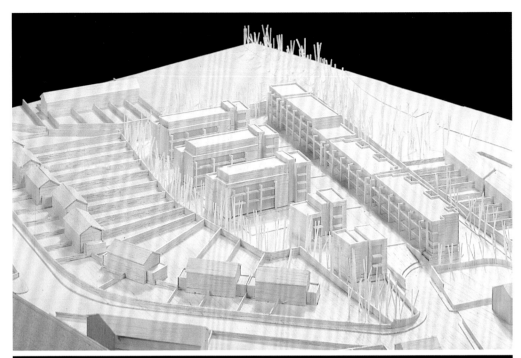

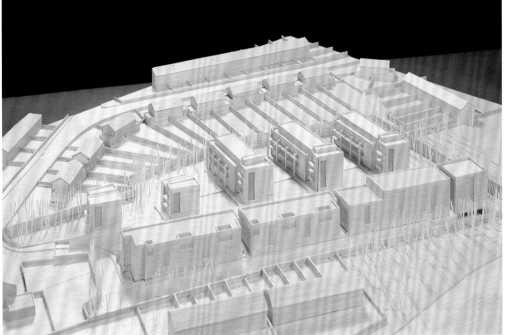

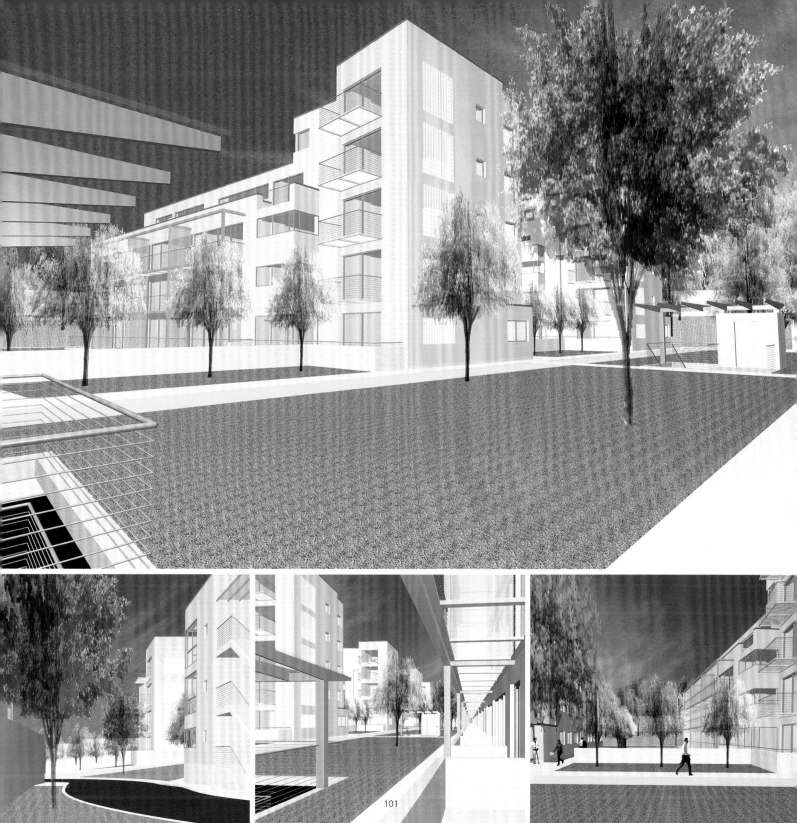

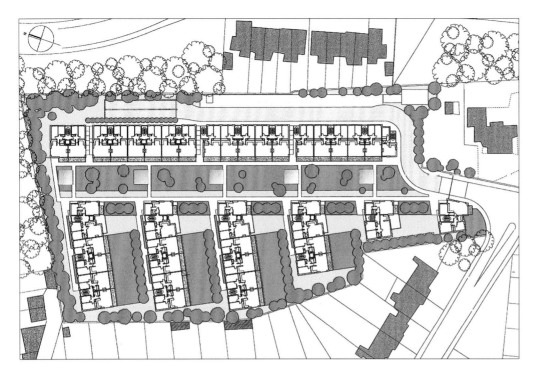

freeing the site to allow the creation of a large landscaped common garden. In tandem with this strategy, the general site level that is being established is substantially lower than that of the surrounding properties. All residents enter their apartments from the common garden. Having parked below ground, access to the garden is provided by means of a light canopy structure containing a staircase and lift. The absence of cars is a unique aspect of the development.

The buildings will be largely finished in brick. The north and eastern side of the blocks (containing the bedrooms) are more wall-like, with punched openings and a further rhythm of glazed staircases. The western and southern elevations consist of a light steel structure of balconies and terraces which will, over time, become inhabited with plants and creepers.

Site plan

Elevation of a south-facing block, section through terrace and underground carpark

Plans (part-plans of 1st, 2nd floors)

opposite

Nearing completion (Summer 2002)

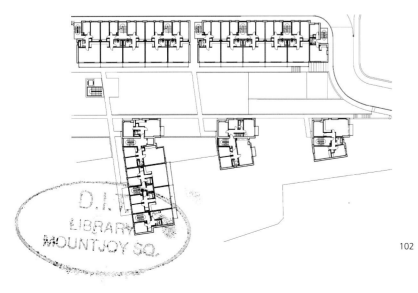

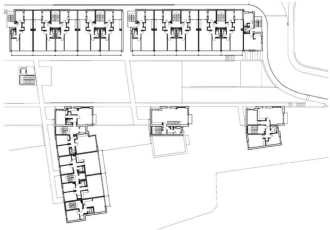

Box House
Sandymount, Dublin 4 (1997-98)

This mews house is to the rear of a two-storey Victorian town house, its corner site having frontage to both the mews lane and the main road. The scheme proposed a two-storey house which would protect the existing amenities of the main house. It achieves this by addressing itself to the main road and to the mews lane. The rear garden of the main house is substantially retained and not overlooked.

The accommodation is arranged around a series of private, external spaces. At ground floor there are two bedrooms, a study, toilet and storage spaces. The entrance is from an external carport/courtyard. A second courtyard to the rear is addressed by the master bedroom and study. At first floor, the living/dining area addresses a large, private, enclosed terrace to the side. This allows the large tree to be retained in the garden and maximises the amount of garden space retained. This arrangement is expressed architecturally as a brick box and a rendered box. There is a special rooflight over the main staircase, and a west light, clad in patinated zinc, over the living room.

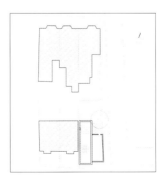

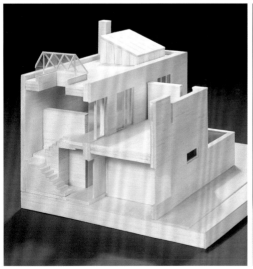

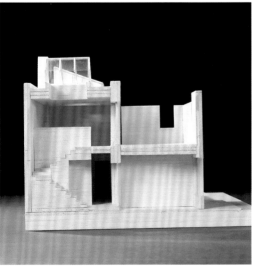

BOX HOUSE

View of house showing upper-floor
'window' to roof terrace

Axonometric

Mews lane and street elevations

opposite

First-floor roof terrace

Views of interior

Plans (ground, 1st floor) and cross-section
showing roof-lit stairwell

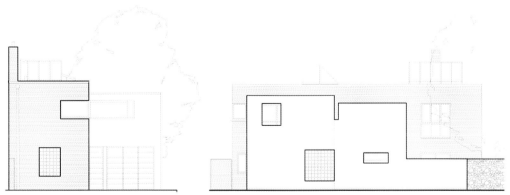

Scoop House
Rathmines, Dublin 6
(1999-2000)

This project is for a three-bedroom house to the rear of an existing 19th-century town house.

The project consists of two interlocking elements – a brick box and a rendered extrusion in an L-shaped configuration. The brick box contains bedrooms at first-floor level. The rendered element sits beneath the brick box and is straddled by it. At ground floor it contains a carport, entry and kitchen. It becomes a double-height dining/living space to the rear, with a curved zinc-clad roof scooping in western light at high level. A special rooflight at the top of the staircase interrupts the curved profile of the roof and allows headroom as one turns onto the gallery leading to the bedroom suite. The volume of the living space is revealed by the casting of light along its surface.

Views of model showing curved roof of living/dining space

opposite

Double-height living space

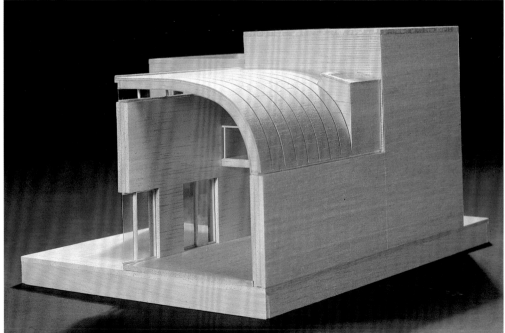

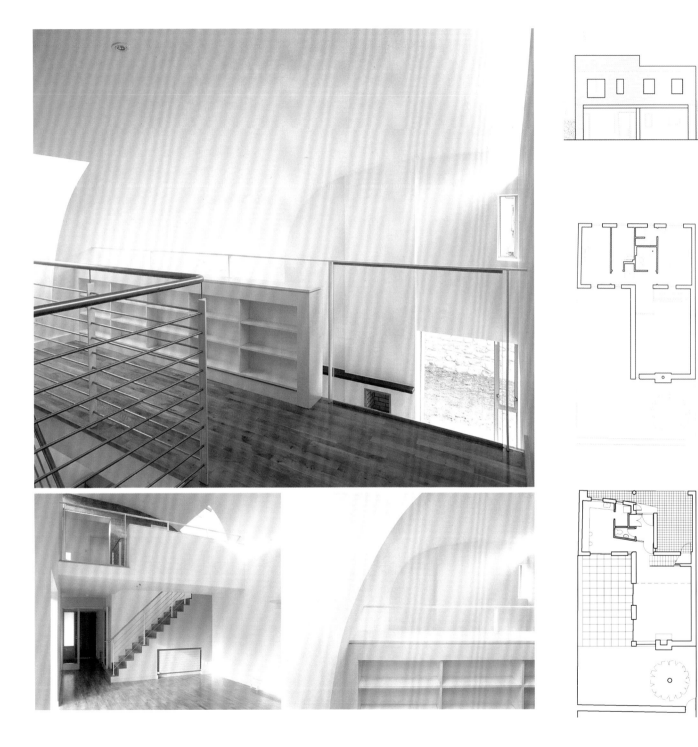

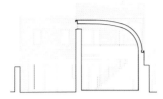

SCOOP HOUSE

Cross-section through living/dining room

View from rear with curved, zinc-clad roof of living space

Long section

Views of entrance on mews lane and courtyard at night

opposite

Views of and from 1st floor gallery

Plans (ground, 1st floors) and elevation to mews lane

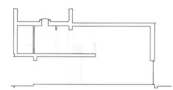

Wall House
Dublin City University (2000-01)

The existing 19th-century lodge is located at the western edge of the campus. It sits in the centre of a rectangular site which is adjacent to the Albert College building. The site is flat and has many trees, particularly at its perimeter. This project restores the building to residential use for the president of the university, and provides new spaces for more formal use in a series of additions.

The accommodation comprises a formal reception room and dining room for corporate entertaining, along with the ancillary uses of holding kitchen, cloakroom and bathroom, a study and a guest suite. This accommodation is provided in a series of single-storey, predominantly glazed pavilions, which, through their disposition on the site, create a number of spaces emanating from the existing building. These proposed outdoor rooms will provide an arrival forecourt, a family garden, a formal lawn space, and a concealed service area, each relating to the appropriate internal room. In this way, the scheme will become an enclave of various spaces and uses, with the historic building as its centrepiece.

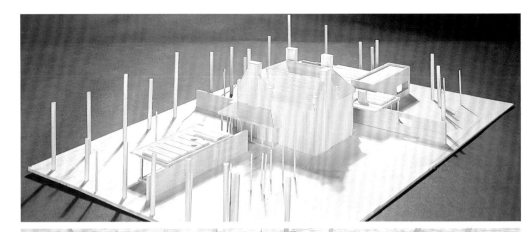

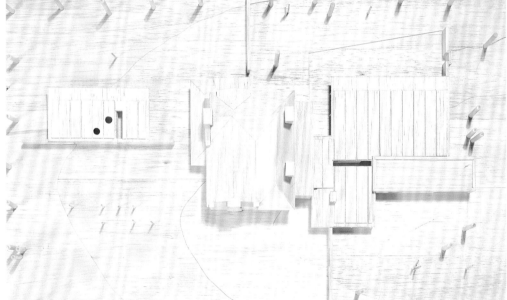

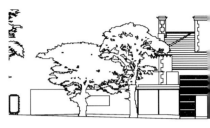

WALL HOUSE

previous pages

Site plan and views of model showing new pavilions to either side of existing house

Formal dining room

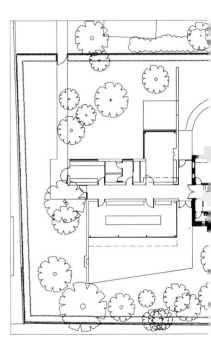

Internal and external views of the project as it neared completion (Spring 2002)

North elevation showing new pavilions to either side of existing house

Ground-floor plan

South elevation

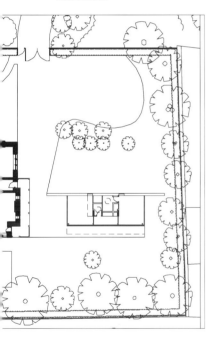

The New Pillar

O'Connell Street, Dublin 1 (1998)
competition entry

The form of our proposal is that of a simple glass tower which is enriched by various surface treatments and markings. It is a straightforward construction of lift and staircase whose primary practical use is to facilitate the viewing of the city.

Its plan dimension is determined by the size of a ten-person lift surrounded by a staircase. It is five metres higher than Nelson's Pillar. Its overall proportions are, therefore, slender and elegant, and its plan matches the dimension of the base of the original structure.

Within this basic organisation, the structure itself has an undercroft and base, a middle and a top. The base comprises a plate-glass enclosure to a height of five metres, sitting on a concourse below street level. The middle comprises a net of stainless steel cables which will receive inscribed clear-glass tiles. The top is a 5m glazed cube 'sky-room' affording panoramic views of the city.

A circular concourse space is located below street level and is accessed by a ramp on one side and by a staircase on the other. The primary motivation to descend before ascending was to create a threshold between the tower and the street. A sense of mystery and anticipation is created by 'leaving' the city before ascending skywards. The ramp and staircase which lead to the concourse are contained in glazed prismatic and jewel-like enclosures embedded in the street. They are entered at the base of the tower. From this concourse the lift goes to the top of

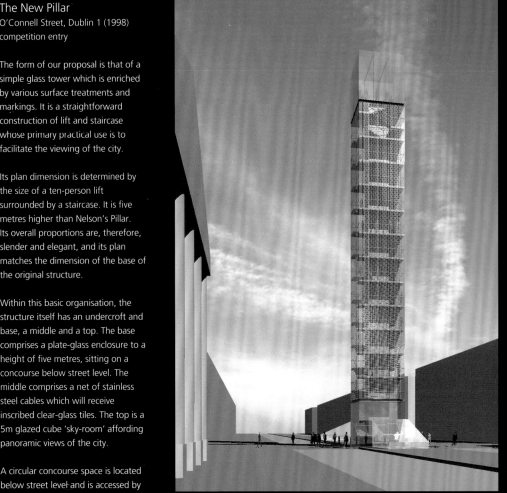

the structure. Most visitors will probably ascend by lift and descend by staircase, enjoying the panorama at the top and the complimentary spiralling descending view of the city on the way down.

The base at street level consists of 5m x 5m plate-glass walls on each side. We propose that etched works be carried out on these walls by an artist from each of the four provinces, selected through competition.

The middle part of the structure is 35m high. It is formed with tensioned stainless steel cables, running horizontally and vertically, to create a 225mm x 225mm net. This net will be infilled with 200mm square clear-glass tiles which people can have inscribed. Individuals, couples, families and school groups have the option of purchasing a tile at concourse level, which provides an opportunity to register their visit and contribute to the completion of the tower. A position on the tower can also be chosen electronically. The glass tile will then be fixed in position at a later date by a trained glass rigger, using standard rivetted storm fixings. When complete, this incredible wall of messages and signs will form a tapestry through which the city is viewed as one descends.

The top is a 'sky room' from which a panoramic view of the city is revealed. It is a 5m cube with glazed walls and roof. Laminated glass fins and beams provide the structure. The roof is fritted to reduce glare and heat gain. A telescope at each side of the room, along with touch-screen monitors, will provide information about particular buildings and landmarks.

Computer model of the new Pillar looking
northwards from the GPO

Cross-section, with portico of GPO

opposite

Façade detail of inscribed, clear-glass tiles
and 'sky room' at top of Pillar

Plan and section through Pillar and
undercroft

A crystalline glass tower

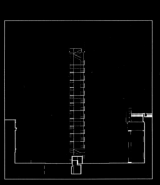

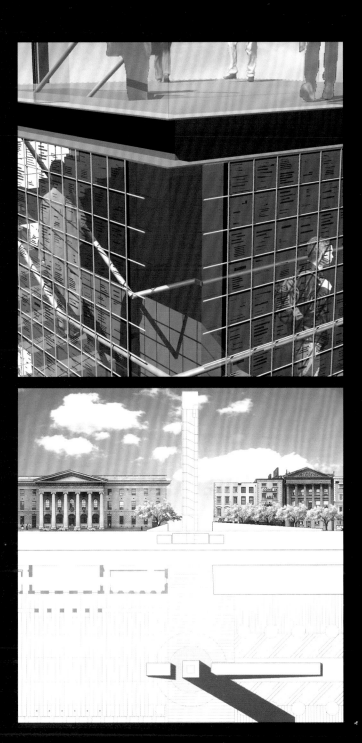

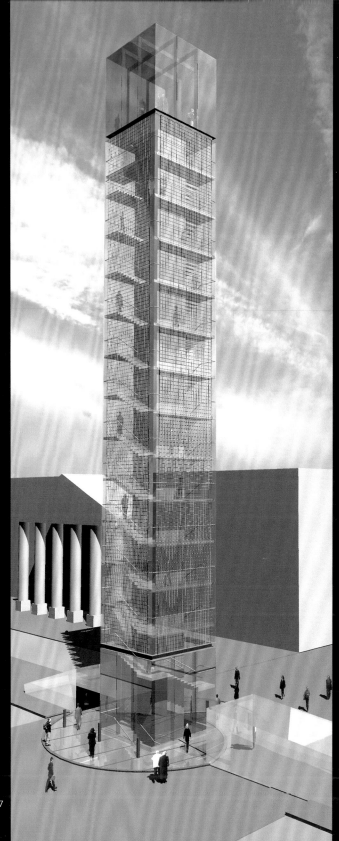

Bars and Restaurant, Point Depot
North Wall Quay, Dublin 1 (1987-88)

The Point Depot was built in 1878 as a goods warehouse for the Great Southern & Western Railways in Dublin's north docklands. The total building is 10,000m² in area, and consists of a cast-iron 'shed' with a formal front to the River Liffey in the shape of a masonry building, 8m deep by 50m long.

This project was part of the overall conversion of the building into a multipurpose concert, exhibition and conference centre. The bar areas consist of two large volumes at either end of an entrance hall, with a mezzanine at gallery level connecting them. This gallery level connects all three spaces axially, and becomes a bridge as it passes through the entrance hall.

The services and lighting in each of the stone-walled spaces are carried on a suspended service platform which acts as another connecting element. All new interventions are consciously precise and polychromatic to contrast with the original stone envelope.

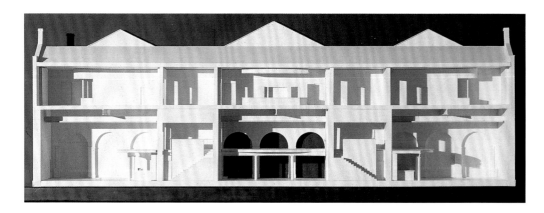

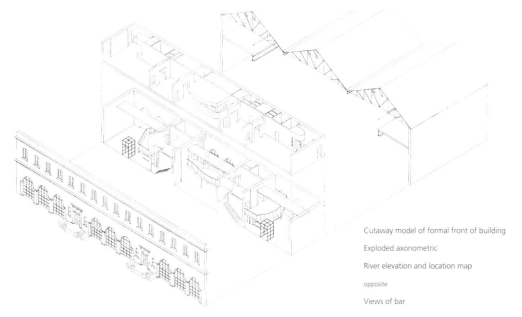

Cutaway model of formal front of building

Exploded axonometric

River elevation and location map

opposite

Views of bar

Harbourmaster Bar
IFSC, Dublin 1 (1998)

The project involved providing additional accommodation for the existing bar at the International Financial Services Centre in Dublin's former docklands. The original building was for the harbour master of the docklands area.

The scheme is two-storey-over-basement. It provides food preparation and general service accommodation below ground, while locating a bar and restaurant overlooking the inner dock on the two upper floors.

The building is a brick box towards the adjoining offices, while the spaces adjacent to the water are fully glazed. Internally, the finishes are a combination of painted plastered walls and dark wood surfaces, with stainless-steel bar fittings.

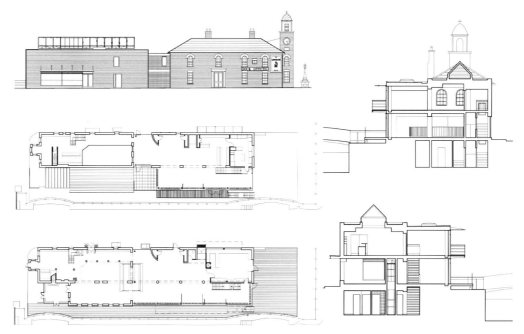

Dockside view

Rear elevation

Plans (ground, 1st floor)

Cross-sections through old and new parts of the complex

opposite

Views of the restaurant area

Rear elevation

interview continued from page 23

denly there is this big release of space. It sits there, and you have all of these surrounding buildings bearing down on you.

Is it a similar release of potential that Curved Street accomplishes within a set of constricted city blocks?

The thing that was very exciting about Temple Bar was making these civic spaces, and then being allowed to make public buildings which would form those spaces. But then the question about Curved Street is whether there is enough happening on it. Should there have been two public buildings forming it, or should Arthouse or the Music Centre have been more part of the fabric? I'm not sure, and I think that applies equally to Meeting House Square. At least Meeting House Square has a restaurant now, which helps to alleviate that tension that public buildings can generate. But I think that the formal moves are very good.

So, in that case, why is Curved Street curved?

Well, it was about these physical configurations that were there. Arthouse also embraces 22 Eustace Street, an existing house, and it was about arriving at a resolution of that which was formally strong. I inherited the site from the Temple Bar Architectural Framework competition. As part of Group 91, I worked on a different part of Temple Bar during the competition, which was the west end. We had a meandering route which went up diagonally across the back of Fishamble Street and had the tower of Christchurch at the end of it, so it was less orthogonal than what has been built.

Typically in Temple Bar, brick is for ordinary buildings, whereas cultural buildings must have your stone or 'white stuff'.

Well the Project is blue and silver. Blue instead of stone. Essentially I didn't want to do another white building. Also I was afraid that we would be asked to paint it terracotta to blend in with the neighbours, whereas I had always felt that this was an important public building and it should be different. The painted render refers back to the early character of Temple Bar, and

you still see a lot of it around. So it's blue, with galvanised metal panels – a simple palette but it's very powerful.

Yet your just-completed Dawson Street office block reverts to a more traditional palette of cream and terracotta, in quite a specific contextual analogy.

I'm very pleased with Dawson Street, with the way it works. Here you basically have a speculative office building – the first time Dublin City Council had ever done this – but the challenge was to see if we could lift such an ordinary programme, make something exciting that still fitted into Dawson Street. I mean, Dawson Street is a great street. Nearly every building is different architecturally, and it has its special pieces – the Mansion House, St Anne's church and the Royal Irish Academy. It also has a certain width and scale, and I think people really enjoy it.

So we took the opportunity to make these changes to the fenestration of the building – the large windows to the front, the saw-tooth windows to the side – and then we made the set-back to the upper storey, all in response to the complexities of the urban condition. I think, because of this, one could really imagine a life within the building, even though there's no inside as such – we've had to leave that to the tenants. And I think that the colours work – the cream limestone and the red sandstone to the street increases the perception of depth of the site and breaks down the scale of the building. Just by manipulating the colour of the materials I think it works really well.

Do you have a particular philosophy of colour? I detect touches of Steven Holl's spatial colour reflection in Kildare Street.

It isn't so much about colour, more about light. Holl relies on creating an artificial landscape using reflected artificial light. In the Scoop House, the idea of making that curved roof was that in the summer that whole curved surface is filled with natural light from the west-facing slot window. I'd like to try to develop forms in the work that are more responsive to those kinds of things. That comes back to what I was saying about Blackrock, for instance. I could imagine doing a project six or seven years on which had a similar starting point, which was this elemental scheme, but the elements might be more in response to the

New Galleries, Irish Museum of Modern Art,
Dublin (1995-99)

Wall House, Dublin City University
(2000-01)

internal spatial characteristics that you want to create through the use of light, rather than just being forms, or having a relationship with familiar forms.

Using light as the positive material?

That's right. I'm still interested in elemental projects, but the quality of the forms might be more informed by considerations of light or spatial characteristics. I feel that I'm only just starting to think about modelling light properly. I think it could be much more 'manufactured' and more about revealing surfaces.

But there's an excitement there about seeing your work built, which I'm sure is growing all the time.

I think the privilege of making architecture is just amazing when you contemplate it. When working with Declan McGonagle on IMMA, he used a phrase which I like, that you make 'a new reality' when you're building. When you're making architecture you are trying to make a new reality.

What do you feel is the new reality?

I think it's about new possibilities, the possibility of modern architecture is to release the potential of things in a different way.

That's why I'm very fond of the New Galleries at IMMA. We are drawing people around the side of the building and making a new front and a new courtyard with an underground room – a walled enclosure. Because of the context, with the formal gardens beyond, I really feel excited when standing on that terrace, where nobody ever stood before. Relating the formal gardens and the Deputy Master's House in that way, using this courtyard, which isn't just a courtyard, but the roof of something else. And yet the whole thing is very still. The black walls are so absorbent you can't even photograph them properly, yet when you're there they're very powerful – powerful but understated. We've added another external room to the museum, and you can now journey around the grounds in a way that wasn't possible before.

The Wall House at Dublin City University and the education centre at Ballyvourney elaborate on what was hinted at in the Deputy Master's House, namely the walled garden.

Its a very potent device to use. It allows you to order the setting for the building and to create outdoor rooms. The Wall House has a pinwheel plan where you get these L-shaped walls which order the whole project. I think it was important to keep back from the main [existing] house, so we set up this series of 'wings', if you like, and the accommodation is then balanced between the public reception room and formal dining room, and the private guest house and study, which, unfortunately, looks like it may not get built. But the walls are treated like garden walls and the whole scheme is single-storey, which reinforces the idea of a garden where you get different pavilions – one public and one smaller private one – with the existing two-storey house at its centre of gravity.

You have set up this kind of plan, but then chosen to consciously define the 'field' by use of a Copper Beech hedge.

As in Ballyvourney [National Centre for Irish Language Education], where the site is defined by a border of trees, and then you get this long building which stretches out and colonises the site.

This is also a wall project.

I have always been interested in wall projects. Kildare Street, for example, used an existing wall as a backdrop with elements set against it. With Ballyvourney we get to make a wall in a natural landscape. In front of the wall we placed a pavilion, which is weighted at one end by a single large volume – also a recurring theme in my work. So it is about reading this wooded setting which contains a pavilion perched lightly on the site. We changed the roof section so that the roof now projects out from the building much more in order to reinforce that floating quality, so you get that quality in section as well as elevation. The pavilion is then anchored by the timber-clad wall, which has a structural thickness, containing services and offices. I think it is important that this wall is open-ended because it is that device which allows it to sit lightly on the site.

This open-endedness is intriguing. It has Modernist references. Even the architectural language is more classically Modern, although the use of timber as a rain-screen in the woods seems almost ironic.

I am using timber here in quite a different way, which is an experiment for me. In this particular context it reinforces the overall concept of the pavilion. 2 x 1 metre panels of Spanish timber veneer with bakelite on the back are positioned as a rain-screen with gaps between, which hopefully reinforces the idea of lightness, of a pavilion. I suppose it is a new direction for me. New directions are opening up and I don't necessarily know where they are leading.

Has your method of working affected how you approach these questions?

Well, I work in a very instinctive way. I don't do a huge amount of measured drawings anymore – more doodles and sketches – but I tend to arrive at the basis for a scheme fairly quickly because I will have been thinking about it for a long time beforehand.

What's important to me is that I'm really trying to make work which is authentic. I want to make work essentially for my own place, drawing on and developing the traditions of modern architecture and a modern way of making space. It's very hard to know how the public perceives your work because you, as the author, are always conscious of the concept behind it, and therefore it is hard to regard it as 'found'. That's why it's the greatest compliment when somebody takes a building for granted – you know, the kind of secret work of architecture where nobody has any idea about the effort you've gone to to make it because it just seems so completely natural and inevitable. I think the most moving things are essentially simple and sure. If there's nothing left to strip away and it's still really powerful, then you're looking at a successful piece of work.

Simon Walker is an architectural graduate of UCD. In private practice since 1996, he has worked as a curator and an architectural critic.

Continuity and Modern Architecture

EDWARD JONES

For Shay Cleary and his generation, the heroic period of modern architecture and the urban qualities of the existing city have been held in equally high esteem. For some this would suggest a fundamental contradiction between the city conceived as a series of discrete objects, and the city in which voids of public space are subtracted from an otherwise continuous texture. Despite the banality of the resulting environments, the city of modern architecture and its preoccupation with objects has been said to reflect the democracy of modern times. Conversely, the promotion of the spatial hierarchy of the traditional city suggests a reactionary position in which the vigour and possibilities of twentieth-century life are suppressed and the old certainties prevail.

If the negative logic of this Zeitgeist argument is to be further pursued we have a condition that is not entirely unfamiliar. On the one hand the existing city takes on a taxidermist mentality with the dead hand of historical correctness firmly at the helm; on the other hand, outside the city walls it is open season.

Here in so-called Edge City, the architect has been sent out to play with his troublesome and nonconformist will to form. Here the normal, familiar, and, dare one say, desirable conditions of urban life no longer apply. Instead, object buildings are randomly situated in a spatial neutrality. Like mad dogs howling at the moon, they hope to draw some attention to themselves. This caricature has produced an unfortunate but entirely predictable polarisation in recent architectural production, in which either the tyranny of 'context' or a mindless free expression are the order of the day.

The work of Shay Cleary resolutely takes up this challenge, and suggests that modern architecture and the requirements of the existing city are not necessarily incompatible. From an impressive portfolio of projects, principally on the city over the last decade, three stand out in their attempt to reconcile this new-architecture-old-city paradox.

The first is the modest but effective transformation of the historic Royal Hospital at Kilmainham into the Irish Museum of Modern Art in 1990. Here, Clearly resurfaced the central courtyard – the first 'room' of the museum – with gravel and stone markings which indicate the new entrance hall positioned centrally on the south side of the court. He then inserted a finely crafted steel and glass staircase painted white in contrast to the stone exterior. The double volume of the staircase connects the two principal levels of the museum, and establishes a clear distinction between new and old. There is no sign of the dead hand of heritage here. All the perimeter galleries focus on the central courtyard, which provides a new venue for various artistic installations. (O'Donnell and Tuomey's Irish Pavilion of 1991 was a particularly memorable addition to this now urbane and flexible public space.) It is interesting to note that as recently as the 1970s, this courtyard at Kilmainham remarkably acted as a repository for all the extant statues of Queen Victoria in Ireland. That these last relics of the Empire should be replaced by the polemics of modern art gives the whole an extra frisson.

Secondly, two projects in Dublin's Temple Bar more explicitly demonstrate Cleary's commitment to the language of modern architecture in the service of restructuring the city. The collaborative urban design enterprise on Temple Bar was by Group 91, a like-minded team of young architects who were students together at University College Dublin in the 1970s, and of which Cleary was a founder-member. By any standards this was a remarkable urban design initiative. It demonstrated that by observing the structure, scale and typologies of the city, the superficies of historical appearances was not an issue. Next door, casting its shadow like a great scarecrow over Temple Bar is the Central Bank, demonstrating *in extremis* the new-architecture-old-city dilemma. In the context of Dublin, if ever the high-minded conservationists were given their key witness for the prosecution this was it. Interestingly, this urban faux pas also provided Group 91 with a compelling example of what not to do.

By way of contrast, Cleary's Arthouse project forms a new curved street, completes an existing urban block, establishes a conventional building height, and maintains continuity with the adjacent area. All very diplomatic, really. The character, appearance and the dynamic interior volumes of this project, however, are those of modern architecture, and in their audacious way do not conform to the stylistic expectations of the contextual approach.

Further to the west, the Project Art Centre replaces previous accommodation on the same site. Here again, Cleary maintains the conventions of the existing city. The appearance this time is of a vibrant blue (Yves Klein) which contrasts strongly with the red brick of the Victorian neighbours. By this, it simultaneously identifies itself as a public place, a building of its own time, and a participant in the continuity of the city.

One looks forward to the realisation of other projects from this impressive portfolio – a portfolio that manages to confront, oppose, and successfully reverse the observation that whilst modern architecture has produced fine free-standing buildings, it has been conspicuously less successful in coming to terms with the existing city. The work offers a welcome and timely alternative to the contemporary and all-pervasive international freak show as the inspiration for the regeneration of our cities.

Edward Jones is a partner in Dixon Jones Architects, London. He has lectured widely and his work has been published internationally.

Selected Buildings and Projects, 1987-2002

IRISH MUSEUM OF MODERN ART
Shay Cleary, Brian McClean, Dominic Stevens, Simon Walker
client: Irish Museum of Modern Art / Office of Public Works

ARTHOUSE, TEMPLE BAR
Shay Cleary, Brian McClean, Aoife O'Donnell, Eilís O'Donnell
client: Temple Bar Properties

WALSALL GALLERY (COMPETITION)
Shay Cleary, Peter Tansey, Brian McClean, Fergal Doyle

**NEW GALLERIES,
IRISH MUSEUM OF MODERN ART**
Shay Cleary, Cormac Allen, Tiernan McCarthy, Mark Elliott, Eoin Healy
client: Irish Museum of Modern Art / Office of Public Works

EXTENSION TO NATIONAL GALLERY OF IRELAND (COMPETITION)
Shay Cleary, Brian McClean, Seamus Thornton

PROJECT ARTS CENTRE, TEMPLE BAR
Shay Cleary, Brian McClean, Cormac Allen, Kathleen Creed, Carlus Buckley, Adam Peavoy, Kevin Woods
client: Temple Bar Properties / Project Arts Centre

**MEETING & CONFERENCE FACILITIES,
DEPT OF AGRICULTURE**
Shay Cleary, Brian McClean
client: Office of Public Works

OFFICE BUILDING, DAWSON STREET
Shay Cleary, Tiernan McCarthy, Karen Brownley, Carlus Buckley, Philip Comerford, Stephen Doherty, Tom Larkin, Kevin Woods
client: Dublin City Council

TOWER BUILDING, GRAND CANAL QUAY
Shay Cleary, Mark Elliott, Adam Peavoy, Philip Comerford, Andrew Clancy, Stephen Doherty, Stephen Musiol, Kevin Woods
client: Treasury Holdings Ltd

REDEVELOPMENT AND EXTENSION TO CORK COUNTY HALL
Shay Cleary, David King-Smith, Dermot McCabe, Marcus Lassan, Andrew Clancy, Philip Comerford, Stephen Doherty, Mark Monaghan, Suzannah Potts, Kevin Woods, Melanie O'Reilly, Stephen Musiol
client: Cork County Council

BLACKROCK EDUCATION CENTRE
Shay Cleary, Seamus Thornton
client: Department of Education and Science

NAVAN EDUCATION CENTRE
Shay Cleary, Mark Elliott, Des Twomey
client: Department of Education and Science

LAOIS EDUCATION CENTRE
Shay Cleary, Mark Elliott, Jonathan Garvey, Caroline Lawlor
client: Department of Education and Science

**SCIENCE OF MATERIALS BUILDING,
TRINITY COLLEGE (COMPETITION)**
Shay Cleary, Dominic Stevens, Brian McClean

CENTRE FOR IRISH LANGUAGE EDUCATION, BALLYVOURNEY
Shay Cleary, Kathleen Creed, Dermot McCabe, Tom Larkin, Birgit Sunkel, Kevin Woods
client: Department of Education and Science

MAKING A MODERN STREET
Shay Cleary, Brian McClean

QUEEN STREET HOUSING
Shay Cleary, Seamus Thornton, Brian McClean, David King-Smith, Adam Peavoy, Kathleen Creed, Andrew Clancy, Peter Carroll, Fergal Doyle, Eoin Healy, Steve Larkin, Tom Larkin, Melanie O'Reilly, Kevin Woods
client: Dublin City Council

**APARTMENT DEVELOPMENT,
GLANDORE ROAD**
Shay Cleary, David King-Smith, Dermot McCabe, Andrew Walsh, Stephen Musiol, Kevin Woods
client: PJ Walls / Morrisson JV

BOX HOUSE, SANDYMOUNT
Shay Cleary, Tiernan McCarthy, Jonathan Garvey, Des Twomey, Kevin Woods

SCOOP HOUSE, RATHMINES
Shay Cleary, Tiernan McCarthy, Kevin Woods

WALL HOUSE, DUBLIN CITY UNIVERSITY
Shay Cleary, Kathleen Creed, Stephen Doherty, Birgit Sunkel, Kevin Woods
client: Dublin City University

BARS AND RESTAURANT, POINT DEPOT
Shay Cleary, John Dorman, Eilís O'Donnell, Esmonde O'Brien
client: Henry A Crosbie

PILLAR COMPETITION
Shay Cleary, Tim McFarlane (Dewhurst McFarlane), David King-Smith, Kevin Woods

HARBOURMASTER BAR, IFSC
Shay Cleary, Tiernan McCarthy, Eoin Healy, Kevin Woods
client: Thomas Read Group

SHAY CLEARY

1951	Born in Cork
1969-74	University College Dublin (BArch)
1974	Marcel Breuer Architecte, Paris
1975	Candilis Josic & Woods, Paris
1976	Neave Browne, London Borough of Camden
1977-96	Design Tutor, School of Architecture, UCD
1978-80	Partner, Grafton Architects
1980-81	President, Architectural Association of Ireland
1981-86	Cleary & Hall Architects
1987	Established Shay Cleary Architects
	Member, Royal Institute of the Architects of Ireland
1989	Visiting Critic, Princeton University, NJ, and
	Royal College of Art, London
1991-97	Director, Group 91 Architects
1998	Fellow, Royal Institute of the Architects of Ireland

SELECTED BUILDINGS AND PROJECTS

2000-	AN tIONAD NÁISIÚNTA OIDEACHAIS GAEILGE, Ballyvourney, Co Cork
2000-01	WALL HOUSE, Dublin City University
1999-	CORK COUNTY HALL, Redevelopment and Extension (competition winner)
1999-02	TOWER BUILDING, Grand Canal Quay, Dublin
1999-00	SCOOP HOUSE, Rathmines, Dublin
1998-02	APARTMENT DEVELOPMENT, Glandore Road, Dublin OFFICE BUILDING, Dawson Street, Dublin (RIAI Regional Award, 2002)
1998-00	NAVAN EDUCATION CENTRE, Co Meath
1998	HARBOURMASTER BAR, International Financial Services Centre, Dublin

Shay Cleary has been in private practice since 1978 when he established Grafton Architects with Yvonne Farrell, Shelley McNamara, Tony Murphy and Frank Hall. From 1981 to 1986 he practiced as Cleary & Hall with Frank Hall. In 1987 he established Shay Cleary Architects. He was a founder-member of Group 91 Architects who won the international competition for the redevelopment of Temple Bar. He lives in Dublin with his wife Lulu, his sons Ben and Oliver, and his daughter Annabel.

THE NEW PILLAR, O'Connell Street, Dublin (project)

1997-98 BOX HOUSE, Sandymount, Dublin

1996-00 PROJECT ARTS CENTRE, Temple Bar, Dublin
(AAI Award 2001)

1996-98 LAOIS EDUCATION CENTRE, Portlaoise

1996 EXTENSION TO NATIONAL GALLERY OF IRELAND,
Clare Street, Dublin (invited competition)

1995- QUEEN STREET HOUSING, Dublin

1995-99 NEW GALLERIES, IRISH MUSEUM OF MODERN ART,
Royal Hospital Kilmainham, Dublin
(special mention, AAI Awards 2001)

1995 SCIENCE OF MATERIALS BUILDING, Trinity College,
Dublin (invited competition)
WALSALL ART GALLERY, England
(competition, 2nd stage)

1994-96 BLACKROCK EDUCATION CENTRE, Dun Laoghaire,
Co Dublin (RIAI Regional Awards commendation, 1997;
special mention, AAI Awards 1997)

1993-94 DEPT OF AGRICULTURE, Meeting and Conference
Facilities, Kildare Street, Dublin
(special mention, AAI Awards 1995)

1992-95 ARTHOUSE, Temple Bar, Dublin
(RIAI Regional Award, 1997; special mention, AAI Awards
1997; shortlisted as part of Temple Bar Framework Plan,
Mies van der Rohe Award, 1997)

1991 TEMPLE BAR FRAMEWORK PLAN, Group 91
Architects (competition winner)
MAKING A MODERN STREET, Group 91 (project)

1990-91 IRISH MUSEUM OF MODERN ART, Royal Hospital
Kilmainham, Dublin
(RIAI Regional Award, 1992; AAI Award, 1992)

1987-88 POINT DEPOT, Bars and Restaurant, National
Exhibition Centre, Dublin (AAI Downes Medal, 1989)

SELECTED EXHIBITIONS

2002 *Shay Cleary Architects – Projects and Buildings
1987-2001*, RIAI Architecture Centre, Dublin
AAI Awards 2001, RIAI Architecture Centre, Dublin

1998 *Competitions*, RIAI Architecture Centre, Dublin

1997-98 *20th Century Architecture: Ireland*, Deutsches
Architektur-Museum, Frankfurt; RIBA, London; RHA
Gallagher Gallery, Dublin

1996 *Temple Bar – The Power of an Idea*, Temple Bar
Properties, Dublin
Building on the Edge of Europe, l'Imaginaire Irlandais
festival, Maison d'Architecture, Paris

1991 *Making a Modern Street* (Group 91 Architects),
Riverrun Gallery, Dublin; Architektur Forum, Zurich;
Irish Museum of Modern Art, Dublin

1986 *European Architects: A New Generation*,
Architectural Association, London

COLLABORATORS (since 1987)

Cormac Allen, Dermot Boyd, Karen Brownley, Carlus Buckley,
Peter Carroll, Andrew Clancy*, Peter Cody, Philip Comerford,
Martin Cox, Kathleen Creed, Stephen Doherty, Marcus
Donaghy, John Dorman, Feargal Doyle, Mark Elliott (associate),
Jennifer Fay, Sam Gaine, Jonathan Garvey, Ronan Halpenny,
Eoin Healy, Anne Henry, Hugh Kelly, David King-Smith
(associate), Steve Larkin, Tom Larkin*, Marcus Lassan*, Dermot
McCabe*, Tiernan McCarthy (associate), Brian McClean
(associate), Jesmond Meli, Mark Monaghan*, Stephen Musiol*,
Esmonde O'Briain, Aoife O'Donnell, Eilís O'Donnell, Antoinette
O'Neill, Melanie O'Reilly*, Adam Peavoy*, Suzannah Potts*,
Dominic Stevens, Birgit Sunkel, Peter Tansey, Seamus Thornton,
Des Tuomey, Simon Walker, Andrew Walsh, Brian Ward, Kevin
Woods*

Administration – Aoife Cox*, Catherine Moran*, Sinéad Pickett,
Lesley-Anne Whelan, Niamh Redmond, Nicola Masterson*

*current office

SHAY CLEARY ARCHITECTS
18 Palmerston Park, Rathmines, Dublin 6
tel: +353 (0)1 4972311 / fax 01-4973053
e-mail: info@sca.ie / web-site: www.sca.ie

GANDON EDITIONS

Gandon Editions is the leading producer of books on Irish art and architecture. Established in 1983, it was named after the architect James Gandon (1743-1823) as the initial focus was on architecture titles. We now produce 20 art and architecture titles per year, both under the Gandon imprint and on behalf of a wide range of art and architectural institutions in Ireland. We have produced over 250 titles to date. Gandon books are available from good bookshops in Ireland and abroad, or direct from:

GANDON EDITIONS
Oysterhaven, Kinsale, Co Cork, Ireland

tel	+353 (0)21-4770830
fax	+353 (0)21-4770755
e-mail	gandon@eircom.net
web-site	www.gandon-editions.com

PROFILES

In 1996, Gandon Editions launched PROFILES – a series of medium-format books on contemporary Irish artists. In 1997, we launched ARCHITECTURE PROFILES – a companion series on contemporary Irish architects. Both series are edited and designed by John O'Regan. Each volume in the PROFILES series carries two major texts – a critical essay and an interview with the artist / architect – and is comprehensively illustrated in colour. In response to demand from readers, we have now expanded the pagination and colour content of both series, and introduced an international subscription service.

Profile 1 – PAULINE FLYNN
essays by Paul M O'Reilly and Gus Gibney
ISBN 0946641 722   Gandon Editions, 1996
48 pages   22 illus (incl 19 col)   €10 pb

Profile 2 – SEÁN McSWEENEY
essay by Brian Fallon; interview by Aidan Dunne
ISBN 0946641 862   Gandon, Winter 2002
(2nd revised and expanded ed; 1st ed, 1996)
60 pages   col illus   €10 pb

Profile 3 – EILÍS O'CONNELL
essay by Caoimhín Mac Giolla Léith; interview by Medb Ruane
ISBN 0946641 870   Gandon Editions, 1997
48 pages   35 illus (incl 27 col)   €10 pb

Profile 4 – SIOBÁN PIERCY
essay by Aidan Dunne; interview by Vera Ryan
ISBN 0946641 900   Gandon Editions, 1997
48 pages   38 illus (incl 32 col)   €10 pb

Profile 5 – MARY LOHAN
essay by Noel Sheridan; intro and interview by Aidan Dunne
ISBN 0946641 889   Gandon Editions, 1998
48 pages   22 illus (incl 21 col)   €10 pb

Profile 6 – ALICE MAHER
essay and interview by Medb Ruane
ISBN 0946641 935   Gandon Editions, 1998
48 pages   29 illus (incl 23 col)   €10 pb

Profile 7 – CHARLES HARPER
essay by Gerry Walker; interview by Aidan Dunne; afterword by Bob Baker
ISBN 0946846 111   Gandon Editions, 1998
48 pages   24 illus (incl 19 col)   €10 pb

Profile 8 – MAUD COTTER
essay and interview by Luke Clancy
ISBN 0946846 073   Gandon Editions, 1998
48 pages   30 illus (incl 24 col)   €10 pb

Profile 9 – MICHEAL FARRELL
essay by Aidan Dunne; intro and interview by Gerry Walker
ISBN 0946846 138   Gandon Editions, 1998
48 pages   33 illus (incl 25 col)   €10 pb

Profile 10 – BARRIE COOKE
intro by Seamus Heaney; essay by Aidan Dunne;
interview by Niall MacMonagle
ISBN 0946846 170   Gandon Editions, 1998
48 pages   29 illus (incl 25 col) €10 pb

Profile 11 – VIVIENNE ROCHE
essay by Ciarán Benson; intro and interview by
Aidan Dunne
ISBN 0946846 235   Gandon Editions, 1999
48 pages   39 illus (incl 30 col) €10 pb

Profile 12 – JAMES SCANLON
essay by Aidan Dunne; interview by Shane
O'Toole; afterword by Mark Patrick Hederman
ISBN 0946641 579   Gandon Editions, 2000
48 pages   51 illus (incl 37 col) €10 pb

Profile 13 – TONY O'MALLEY
essay by Peter Murray; intros by Jay Gates, Jean
Kennedy Smith
ISBN 0946846 456   Gandon Editions, 2000
48 pages   30 illus (incl 26 col) €10 pb

Profile 14 – ANDREW KEARNEY
essay by Simon Ofield; interview by Aoife
Mac Namara; intro by Mike Fitzpatrick
ISBN 0946846 74X   Gandon Editions, 2001
60 pages   83 illus (incl 69 col) €10 pb

Profile 15 – BERNADETTE KIELY
essay by Aidan Dunne; interview by Jo Allen;
afterword by Ciarán Benson
ISBN 0946846 804   Gandon Editions, 2002
60 pages   41 illus (incl 35 col) €10 pb

Profile 16 – ANNE MADDEN
essay and interview by Aidan Dunne
ISBN 0946846 863   Gandon Editions, 2002
60 pages   42 illus (incl 37 col) €10 pb

Profile 17 – ANDREW FOLAN
essay by Paul O'Brien; intro and interview by
Patrick T Murphy
ISBN 0946641 919   Gandon Editions, 2002
60 pages   57 illus (incl 46 col) €10 pb

Profile 18 – JOHN SHINNORS
essay by Brian Fallon; intro and interview by
Aidan Dunne
ISBN 0946846 782   Gandon Editions, 2002
60 pages   51 illus (incl 49 col) €10 pb

Profile 19 – CAMILLE SOUTER
essay by Brian Fallon; interview by Niall
MacMonagle
ISBN 0946846 91X   Gandon, Winter 2002
60 pages   col illus €10 pb

ARCHITECTURE PROFILES

Profile 1 – O'DONNELL + TUOMEY
interview by Kester Rattenbury; texts by Hugh
Campbell, Kevin Kieran, Robert Maxwell, Wilfried
Wang, Williams & Tsien
ISBN 0946641 986   Gandon Editions, 1997
48 pages   64 illus (incl 27 col) €10 pb

Profile 2 – McGARRY NíÉANAIGH
essay by Raymund Ryan; interview by
Dermot Boyd
ISBN 0946641 994   Gandon Editions, 1997
48 pages   56 illus (incl 26 col) €10 pb

Profile 3 – GRAFTON ARCHITECTS
essays by Hugh Campbell, Kenneth Frampton,
Elizabeth Hatz; interview by Raymund Ryan
ISBN 0946846 057   Gandon Editions, 1999
60 pages   131 illus (incl 86 col) €10 pb

Profile 4 – SHAY CLEARY
essay by Raymund Ryan; interview by Simon
Walker; afterword by Edward Jones
ISBN 0946846 898   Gandon Editions, 2002
132 pages   col illus €20 pb

title in preparation: McCULLOUGH MULVIN
to be continued ...

*note: details of forthcoming volumes correct at
time of going to press but are liable to change*